CAMBRIDGE LIBRARY COLLECTION

Books of enduring scholarly value

Linguistics

From the earliest surviving glossaries and translations to nineteenth-century academic philology and the growth of linguistics during the twentieth century, language has been the subject both of scholarly investigation and of practical handbooks produced for the upwardly mobile, as well as for travellers, traders, soldiers, missionaries and explorers. This collection will reissue a wide range of texts pertaining to language, including the work of Latin grammarians, groundbreaking early publications in Indo-European studies, accounts of indigenous languages, many of them now extinct, and texts by pioneering figures such as Jacob Grimm, Wilhelm von Humboldt and Ferdinand de Saussure.

An Indian Glossary

T.T. Roberts, an East India Company lieutenant attached to a native regiment, published this glossary in 1800 to assist those newly arrived in India. Roberts's guide was to Indian terms which had already entered into common use among the English in India, rather than material to help Europeans to study Indian languages in depth (which was the purpose of the East India Company's Fort William College in Calcutta, founded in the same year). English did not become the dominant language of administration until the 1830s, and even then many Indian and Persian words continued to be widely used. Arranged alphabetically, Roberts's glossary contains over one thousand entries, from personal names and titles to terms relating to food, drink, trade, law and religion. It is a valuable source of information on colonial Indian history, geography and society, with explanations of names, places, and the status of different castes.

Cambridge University Press has long been a pioneer in the reissuing of out-of-print titles from its own backlist, producing digital reprints of books that are still sought after by scholars and students but could not be reprinted economically using traditional technology. The Cambridge Library Collection extends this activity to a wider range of books which are still of importance to researchers and professionals, either for the source material they contain, or as landmarks in the history of their academic discipline.

Drawing from the world-renowned collections in the Cambridge University Library, and guided by the advice of experts in each subject area, Cambridge University Press is using state-of-the-art scanning machines in its own Printing House to capture the content of each book selected for inclusion. The files are processed to give a consistently clear, crisp image, and the books finished to the high quality standard for which the Press is recognised around the world. The latest print-on-demand technology ensures that the books will remain available indefinitely, and that orders for single or multiple copies can quickly be supplied.

The Cambridge Library Collection will bring back to life books of enduring scholarly value (including out-of-copyright works originally issued by other publishers) across a wide range of disciplines in the humanities and social sciences and in science and technology.

An Indian Glossary

Consisting of Some Thousand Words and Terms Commonly Used in the East Indies

T. T. ROBERTS

CAMBRIDGE
UNIVERSITY PRESS

CAMBRIDGE UNIVERSITY PRESS

Cambridge, New York, Melbourne, Madrid, Cape Town, Singapore,
São Paolo, Delhi, Dubai, Tokyo, Mexico City

Published in the United States of America by Cambridge University Press, New York

www.cambridge.org
Information on this title: www.cambridge.org/9781108027052

© in this compilation Cambridge University Press 2010

This edition first published 1800
This digitally printed version 2010

ISBN 978-1-108-02705-2 Paperback

AN

INDIAN GLOSSARY:

CONSISTING OF

SOME THOUSAND WORDS AND TERMS

COMMONLY USED IN THE

EAST INDIES;

WITH

FULL EXPLANATIONS OF THEIR RESPECTIVE MEANINGS.

FORMING AN USEFUL

VADE MECUM,

EXTREMELY SERVICEABLE IN ASSISTING STRANGERS

TO ACQUIRE WITH

EASE AND QUICKNESS

THE

Language of that Country.

By T. T. ROBERTS,

Lieut. &c. of the Third Regt. &c. of the Native Infantry, E. I.

Exempla omnia jacerent in tenebris, nifi literarum lumen accederet.

CIC.

LONDON:

PRINTED FOR MURRAY AND HIGHLEY, FLEET STREET;
STEWART, PICCADILLY; AND COLLINS,
CHANGE ALLEY.

1800.

Printed by S. Gosnell,
Little Queen Street, Holborn.

PREFACE.

IN all attempts to acquire knowledge in any art or fcience, the firft efforts are to make ourfelves mafters of the principles upon which they are founded. Being made converfant with thefe, whatever from thence proceeds, however diffufive, or varioufly diverfified, we can more readily underftand, more perfectly afcertain, and more ftrongly retain in our memory : hence, by a little experience, the whole fubject, however perplexed it may have appeared before, becomes plain and intelligible. For we are empowered to fimplify the whole ; examine it either analytically or fynthetically, tracing it both from caufe to effect, and the reverfe; thus becoming confcious, by the fimilarity of the products, of the certitude of our conclufions.

It happens thus alfo, in our exertions to make ourfelves competent to the underftanding of any language, with which we have been before unacquainted: for, if we look

into works, to the language of which we are entire
ftrangers, the whole appears a compages of letters, hud-
dled together without order or meaning; but no fooner
are we acquainted with the fources from whence it flows,
but we foon acquire the rules by which it is regulated;
our underftanding becomes enlightened, we readily per-
ceive the propriety and beauty of the arrangement, and
our minds are enriched with a number of delightful
ideas.

But let us place ourfelves amongft a fet of foreigners,
whofe language we have not been accuftomed to read
or ever been taught to underftand; their converfation
is to us an unintelligible jargon, as incomprehenfible as
the various tones of the brute creation, each of which
may convey to themfelves a fpecific meaning, but to us
are fo many ufelefs founds.

When I arrived in India, and fome time afterwards,
.I ftood exactly in this unhappy predicament: but what
greatly added to my mortification was, that when I pe-
rufed a newfpaper, that fource of neceffary information,
wherein are frequently inferted very interefting accounts
of various occurrences, which men fearch after with avi-
dity: or, when I looked into works of the authors who
treated of the manners, cuftoms, trade, culture, &c. of
the people, amongft whom it was my prefent lot to re-
fide, my not underftanding a number of the particular

I

terms which were made ufe of, left me, when I had finifhed, as much uninformed as before I began.

From thefe circumftances the fources of all neceffary information were locked up from me; how this evil was to be remedied, became therefore the grand defideratum. After reflecting on the modes of acquiring knowledge, before hinted at, I concluded that the beft method to obviate the difficulty which prefented itfelf to me, as I was at that time divefted of all affiftance, would be to collect every expreffion that was new to me, with which I could meet, and annex the meaning, and thus furnifh myfelf with as large a *copia verborum*, as opportunity might permit, and thefe I fet down as fo many principles, from which I muft derive future information, for higher I could not at prefent move.

I could not continue long inactive. The inquifitive mind, fully bent on inftruction, where knowledge is to be acquired by affiduity and attention, pufhes itfelf rapidly forward in its purfuit, becaufe it is pleafed in its progrefs, and benefited by the refult. I foon, therefore, made an extenfive collection of terms; to thefe I had occafional reference, and thus formed a path through which I received a variety of information, and had the confolatory fatisfaction of experiencing, from day to day, confiderable improvement.

I thought now my labour finifhed; but a new difficulty

ftarted. The terms I had collected were fo numerous, that the conftant references I was obliged to make, became not only troublefome, but tedious, wafting too great a portion of time : to remedy which inconvenience, I digefted the whole into alphabetical order, and thus rendered it extremely ufeful; fo much fo, that reading and converfing furnifhed me with new refources, and became the beneficial as well as agreeable amufement of my leifure hours, fupplying a fund of entertainment, and a relaxation from the feverer duties of my avocation.

Reflecting then on my own fituation, when I firft arrived in India—ftrongly impreffed with the difficulties I had to encounter—experiencing fo much pleafure and fuch great advantage in the conqueft—I was ftruck with the thought, that my labours might be rendered ufeful to thofe who fhould be placed in the fame fituation, and under the like circumftances with myfelf; and might ftimulate others to, and haften the completion of, a fimilar work on a more extenfive fcale. On thefe confiderations I formed a determination to prefent it to the public eye; and notwithftanding a work publifhed by Mr. Hadley, on the fame plan, fell into my hands, I faw no fufficient caufe for dropping the project. Mr. Hadley's work I examined with great care, and found that the terms I had collected, and the explanations I had given, were infinitely more numerous than thofe contained in his edition.

It has been thought right to give this fhort fketch of the motives which induced this publication, that is now launched into the world, unprotected, unpatronized, un-recommended but by the utility which may be rendered to thofe, whofe fortunes may require its aid.

Such then the motives—fuch the intent—the Author flatters himfelf, that the public will receive this little work with candour. Should it, from its utility, be thought worthy of general approbation, he fhall think his la-bour well beftowed, and fhall perfevere in his purfuit with unremitting affiduity to enlarge and improve the work, in order to render a fecond edition, if neceffary, ftill worthy of public countenance and fupport.

THE AUTHOR.

AN

INDIAN GLOSSARY.

A

ABABEERE—caliph—the name fignifies the father of virginity, given becaufe this caliph's daughter alone, of the four wives of Mahomed, was a virgin.

ABBAS SHAH—king of Perfia and founder of a dynafty.

ABBASSIDES—the people of a dynafty.

ABCOORUN—preparation to affault.

ABDALLAH—an Arabic proper name fignifying the flave of God; from *Abd* a flave, and *Allah* God.

ABDALLAH SHAH—a king of the Durannies.

ABDALLIES—a tribe of the Afgans, who are alfo called Durannies—the king was fometimes· incorrectly called *Abdally*, as if it had been the name of a man: his authority extends over Gifni, Candahar, Cabul, Pafhawer, with a part of Alultan and Sind on the fide of Perfia, the greateft part of Karafaun and Sheftaun, and all Bamia on the fide of Tartary.

ABDALRAHIM—a title—the fervant of the provider.

ABDOOSSAMET CAUN—an Abdally—one of the commanders in Coonjepoor.

ABDULCADER—a title—the fervant of the Omnipotent.

ABDULGAFOOR—a title—the fervant of the pardoner.

ABDULRAMAN—a title—the flave of the merciful.

ABEDNEGO—a title—the fervant of righteoufnefs.

B

ABHEIR—a tribe of Hindoos sprung from the connexion of a woman of the *Sooder* with a man of the *Koop*.

ABISS—equal to 1*s*. 4⅓*d*. in Arabia.

ABISSURAS—the name of a king of Bengal.

ABKOORUN—fee *Abcoorun*.

ABOAB or ABUAB—taxes affeffed on the lands over and above the original rent.

ABOAB FOUZDARY, or ABOAB FOUZDARY PERGUNNA—a tax laid on the zemindars by the government, on account of their abolifhing the office of fouzdar (deemed oppreffive), whereby they are obliged to pay equivalent to the amount of the income produced by the taxes of that office.

ABROOA'N—a fort of fine muflin manufactured folely for the ufe of the king's feraglio; a piece of which, cofting four hundred rupees, or 50*l*. fterling, is faid to have weighed only five ficca rupees, and, if fpread upon wet grafs, to have been fcarcely vifible.

ABUBEERE—fee *Ababeere*.

ABULEIS—an epithet—the father of courage.

ABUL FAZL—a title—the father of excellence.

——————a minifter of Akber.

——————a phyfician and hiftorian.

ABULFEDA—an hiftorian—the name fignifies the father of loyalty.

ABULFARAJ—an hiftorian—the name implies the father of the expofitor.

ABUL MAZUFFER—the father of victory—a title.

ABUTALEB—a title—the father of the feeker.

ABYDOS and SESTOS—fortreffes of the Straits—meaning the Dardanelles.

ACHARIGE—a teacher of the Goitre.

ACHBAR NOVEEZ—a writer of news or intelligence.

ACHRAJAT—expenfes, charges, difburfements.

ACRE—a city of Paleftine—the Ptolemais or Afcalon of the ancients, well known on account of the noble defence it made under the conduct of Sir Sidney Smith, againft the repeated affaults upon it by the French General Buonaparte in the year 1799.

ADAULUT—a court of judicature for the trial of caufes refpecting property.

ADAM'S PIKE—a mountain of Ceylon—the natives of the Eaft in general believe that the father of mankind is interred here.

ADDA—a dawk chokey.

ADEETYAS—the offspring of Adeetee—thefe are reckoned twelve, and are nothing more than the emblems of the fun for each month of the year.

ADEW—property that may be given away.

ADHEGEERUN GERRUT—a man who performs ªfervice to his relations.

ADHÂc DOOM—the writer of the Gëetā.

ADHUk—a fmall weight or meafure—four perufts, or four poofkuls.

ADIL—fee *Adul.*

ADONI—a country of India.

ADUL or ADIL—a title—the juft.

AEYSH MAHAL—the place of joy—one of the apartments in the caftle.

AFFUL—aftringent.

AFGANS—the feveral tribes of Mahomedans who inhabit the northern parts of India—there are fome of them fpread all over India, known often by the name of Patans; they are efteemed the beft foldiers in the country.

AG'HA—fir—lord—mafter.

AGHUN—fee *Augun.*

AGNEE—the Hindoo god of fire.

AGNEE ASTER—the Shanfcrit words for fire or *fire-arms,* or weapons of fire—it will no doubt aftonifh thofe who believe Europeans firft found out the means to make gunpowder, that a language of the Eaft, now not fpoken, fhould have terms to exprefs the combuftible and the machine, which is *fhet agnee,* or the weapon which kills a hundred men at once.

AGRA—a town forty-four cofs from Delhi—it is the capital of a province, and formerly the capital of the empire—called alfo *Akbarabad* or the habitation of

Akbar, an appellation given to it in the reign of that emperor.

AHASUERUS—a prince fuppofed to be the fame as Khufroo of the Caianian dynafty of Perfia.

AH, BAUSS-AREE—an exclamation—ufed when in pain or upon the appearance of any thing very alarming.

AHDA—fee *Wada*.

AHDADAR—fee *Wadadar*.

AHEERS—a tribe of Rajapouts.

AHERMAN—the genius of evil.

AHMED—the celebrated.

AHMEDABAD—the capital of the province of Guzerat— fo called from Sultaun Amed, who was king of that province and kept his court in that city: it is two hundred and forty-four meafured cofs from Delhi.

AHMED CAUN BUNGESH—he was created buxy by Gazoodeen Cawn.

AHMEDNAGUR—a confiderable city of the Decan—diftant from Delhi two hundred and eighty meafured cofs; once the capital of the Nizam Shawee fultauns, reduced to the Mogul yoke under Shaw Jehaun, but now under the Mahrattas.

AHMED SHAH—fon of Mahomed Shah—afterwards king of Hindooftan.

AHMEDY—a coin—equal to about a gold mohur.

AHUT—a man pledged for a loan.

AJIM—Perfia—Affyria.

AKASH—a fubtle æther—which the Hindoos fuppofe to be the medium of found; it, in their ideas, forms a fifth element.

AITMAD AL DOWLAT—the fecurity of fortune—a title of Kaffun Beg Cawn.

AJEET SING—fon of the celebrated Jeffwunt Sing, who acted fo capital a part in the competition of Allumgeer and his brothers.

AJMEER—the name of a province.

AKBAR—the comparative of kobir, great—the name of a Mogul emperor.

AKBARABAD—fee *Agra*.

AKBAR NOVEEZ—fee *Achbar noveez*.

AKDANNA—marriage fees received by the cauzy.
AKHERY HESSAB KURCHA—one who adjufts the ac-
counts of the ryots at the end of the year.
AKHERY JUMMA WASSEL BAKY—an aggregate of the
Boorah Jokrah and Akhery Heffab Kurcha's account.
AKHERY NEKHASS—an account formed by the gomafta
or head collector, from the accounts of the currum-
charry.
AKIM—fee *Hakem.*
AKLEEDES—Euclid.
ALADIN—the fublimity of the faith.
ALBANIA—the name of a province.
ALCORAN—the Coran—the book left by Mahomed for
his followers. Al is an Arabic article meaning the.
ALEPPO GUZ—three quarters of a yard in Perfia.
ALI—the fublime.
ALLAHABAD—the capital of a province of that name,
and the place of refidence of the great Mogul during
his continuance under the protection of the Englifh—
it was anciently called *Palibothra.*
ALLUMGEER—one of Aurengzebe's titles—it fignifies
the conqueror of the world.
ALLUMCHUND—a town, ten cofs from Allahabad, on
the road to Cora.
ALLY GOWHER—afterwards Shaw Allum—the prefent
king of Hindooftan, known in Bengal by the name of
Shawzada; he is the fon of Allumgeer the Second.
ALLYGUNGE—a town in the Furruckabad diftrict.
ALLY TIBBAR—means of high defcent.
ALMAGANY—peons ftationed for collections.
AL-MÛGHRIB—the name under which the Afiatics
know Africa—it is fo called from its fituation in the
weft.
ALTUMGAU—an allowance from the revenues as a largefs
to religious men, doctors, and profeffors of fciences.
AMANUT—truft or depofit.
AMANY—in Bahar, denotes lands not rented out, but
remaining in the hands of government.
AMASIA—the name of a province.

AMANRY—a canopied feat for an elephant—an open one is called Howza or Howda.

AMBA RAJAS—affertors of the people's rights—there are fix in the ifland of Mindano who inherit the office.

AMBOUR—the name of a fort.

AMBOYNA—an ifland—which, according to the Arabians, is one of the Maldives.

AMBUSHT, or BADE—a tribe of Hindoos, produced by the connexion of a man of the Bramin, and a woman of the Bice caft; the fhafter of phyfic is given to this tribe.

AMDAUNY—imports.

AMDEHNY—receipts of revenue.

AMEAD BUKSH—the giver of hopes.

AMEEN—fee *Aumeen*.

AMEER, or EMIR UL OMRA—lord of lords, or chief of the nobles—a title beftowed on the buxyulmumalik, or treafurer of the empire.

AMENA—a woman's name.

AMERTO—a place fituated in the province of Bahar.

AMIDA—the name of a city.

AMIR-DAAD—fimilar office to the Englifh lord chief juftice of the pleas.

AMLA—fervant of the governor.

AMREETA, or AMRUT—the water of immortality—the ambrofia of the Hindoo gods.

AMULDAR—fee *Aumil*.

AMULNAMA—fee *Aumulnama*.

ANATOLIA—Afia Minor.

ANCHINA—valuation of the crop.

ANEEBONG—a kind of palm-tree.

ANGOORY—the ifland of grapes.

ANJANGO—the name of a place on the Malabar coaft.

ANNA—the fixteenth part of a rupee.

ANOO PATUK—a falfe accufer—an adulterer—one who, according to the Hindoos, is not orthodox—one who eats with a bafe caft, or murders his friend.

ANOOP SHAHUR, or ANOPSHERE—a Jaut town in the Doab country, on the fouth bank of the Ganges, and north-eaft of the river Jumna, on the borders of Najeb Cawn's country.

ANTAJEE' MANKESEN—a Mahratta general.

ANTY BASHY—an apprentice—a perfon learning any mechanical employment.

ANUSTOFE CHUND—in Shanfcrit poetry, is a line of eight fyllables.

ANUSTOFE CHUND ASHLOGUE—a. regular ftanza of eight fyllables in each of the four lines; this is the moft common afhlogue in the Shanfcrit.

APATERY KURRUM—a fpecies of trifling offences.

APPAJEE—the name of a Mahratta general.

ARAAVE—taxes which have been occafionally impofed to enhance the original land-tax.

ARAM BANU BEGUM—the calm and peaceful princefs—a name.

ARCOT—the capital of a province to which it gives a name, but which is properly called the Carnatic : it is on the eaftern fide of the peninfula: it was not entirely reduced under the Moors till the beginning of this century: it is fometimes called *Muhummud Poor*, the city of *Mahomed Ali*.

ARCOTS—the moft inferior part of genuine rupees, being of lefs value than the ficca rupees by eight per cent.

ARDEBAN—Artabanus.

ARDE KEEL—half wafte land which lies a year or two in fallow.

ARDESHEER BABEGAN—Artaxerxes.

ARDESHEER DERAZ DUST—Artaxerxes Longimanus.

ARIZ MUMALECK—intelligencer of the empire.

ARJOON—the third fon of Pandoo, and the favourite of Kreefhna the Hindoo deity.

ARJUMUND BANU—a title—the noble princefs.

ARNEE—the name of a fort.

ARREIT—a loan.

ARRIB—one hundred crore.

ARRISBEGUY—the perfon who prefents all petitions, either written or by word of mouth.

ARSH—one of the five modes of marriage—it is when

the bridegroom gives the parents of the girl a bull
and cow.

ARSHEEMEDES—Archimedes.

ARSOTTA—a calculated or eftimated account.

ARTE BERUT—a fervant for pecuniary wages.

ARYACHHUND—the irregular ftanzas of the Shanfcrit
poems are always called by this name—but the moft
common method of forming the ftanza is with the
long..line, cabee chhund, and the fhort anufhtofe
chhund alternately, when it bears fome refemblance
to the moft common lyric meafure of the ancients.

ARZAL—an inferior tribe of the Hindoos.

ARZAMIN—a counter-fecurity given to one who is bound
to another in the firft inftance.

ARZEE, or ARZDASHT—a petition or addrefs to the
king—fo called from the two initial letters always
ufed in fuch an addrefs.

ARZEEZ—tin.

ASAM, or ASEM, or ASHAM—the name of a kingdom.

ASBA—relations.

ASCALON—the city now called *Acre*.

ASCUND—the divifion of a work—by us called *book*.

ASHFANIAN—a dynafty of Perfia.

ASHLOGUES—are ftanzas of four lines, in which Shanfcrit poems are generally compofed—they are regular
and irregular.

ASHNAW—purification by bathing.

ASHOO—a horfe of the Turkifh race—which, according
to the Hindoo fcriptures,· performs the journies of
mankind.

ASHORE—one of the three inferior modes of marriage—
in this the man gives money to the father and mother
of the girl he marries as well as to her.

ASHUMMED JUG—a religious ceremony—in which a
horfe is let loofe, which typifies the perfon performing
this facrifice.

ASHWAMMY PIKERY—one who difpofes of another's property without a right to do fo.

ASKANIAN—a dynafty of Perfia.

ASKLAPYOOS—Efculapius.

ASOF JAR—a title—frequently given to vizeers; it fignifies in place or rank of *Afof*, who, it is faid, was Solomon's vizeer.

ASSAM—the fixth month—from the 12th of June to the 13th of July.

ASSAMIES—the name given to thofe merchants employed at Patna, who collect faltpetre from the feveral towns where it is made.

ASSAUMY—a defendant—or any perfon on whom a claim is made.

ASSEL, or ASSEL JUMMA—the original rents with which the lands were firft charged in the books of the empire, exclufive of all additions and impofitions made fince by the government.

ASSEN—the ninth month—from the 14th of September to the 14th of October.

ASSETPOOR—a fmall town in the Rohilla country, reduced by the Mahrattas.

ASSHARS—a Turcoman tribe, divided into two or three clans.

ASSOF—an officer of a veffel.

ASSUD—Sion—a title denoting valour.

ASSUNABAD KOOLBURGA—a city, formerly the capital of the Bamenee fovereigns of Decan.

ASTEER—Efther.

ASUARY—retinue—fee *Sewarry*.

ASWATTHA—the peepal-tree.

ASWEEN and KOOMAR—reputed children of the fun—twins, and phyficians of the gods.

ATALANTIS—this ifland, which is fpoken of by Plato, is called in Afia *Jeezeereh khufhk*—the continental ifland.

ATEE PATUK—inceft.

ATMA—the divine foul.

ATMAMBUNDY—an account fpecifying the number of pergunnas and divifions in a province, the names of the zemindars, and the nature of all feparated lands.

ATTENHEEUH—Athens.

ATTOC—the name of a river that feparates the province of Lahore from Peifhore, the ftream of which is generally fo rapid, that there is but one place where an army can conveniently pafs, and that is defended by a caftle of the fame name: the river and adjoining country is frequently called the *Punjaub* or FiveWaters.

ATTOLON—a province—the name for the thirteen divifions of the Maldives.

AUBDAR KAUNE—the place in which water, &c. &c. are cooled, in ice or faltpetre.

AUDEETYE WAR—Sunday.

AUDALLET—fee *Adaulut.*

AVERRHOES—a phyfician, known by the title *iba refheed,* the fon of the inftructor.

AUGUN—the eleventh month in the Bengal calendar—it commences November 11th, and ends December 10th.

AVICENNA—a phyfician, known under the title of *aboo feena* and aboo-a-ly-feena.

AUMEEN—a fupervifor or officer employed by government to examine and regulate the ftate of the revenues of a diftrict—alfo fometimes an arbitrator or umpire.

AUMIL or AUMILDAR—an officer of the revenues, above an aumeen and a zemindar.

AUMULNAMA—a warrant or order from government, empowering a perfon to take poffeffion of any land.

AURENGABAD—the capital of the province of Dowlatabad—two hundred and fixty-five meafured cofs diftant from Delhi : Aurengzebe had it fo called after his own name, the meaning of which is the City of the Throne.

AURENGZEBE—the name of an emperor of Delhi.

AURUNGS—places where goods are manufactuerd for fale.

AURUT—the Hindooftanee for woman.

AUT GAUM—eight villages.

AYAMMY SHADDY—days of gladnefs—a number of feftival days at the time of marriage among the Hindoos —they begin with the Nandee Mookheh and clofe with the Puntubbee-baden.

AYMA BAZEE REMEEN—lands exempt from payment of revenues, by firmauns of monarchs, but fometimes liable to a fmall quit-rent—they have been generally beftowed for religious purpofes.

2

AYNAA—a name for a particular tenure of free lands.
AYUNOORUS—the holy mountain, Mount Athos—it is called in Turkiſh Jubul-ul-kuſheeſh, or Kuſheſh-taghy, the Mountain of Monks.
AZAZEE AYMA—lands, the grant of which expreſſes one or more entire villages.
AZAZIEL—a name for Satan.
AZEEZOODEN, or YAZAL DIN—Allumgeer the Second.
AZIM, or AZEM—great—glorious.
AZIMABAB—Patna—the capital of Bahar.
AZIM SHAW—great king.
AZIM CAWN—noble lord.
AZIZ MUMALICK—repreſentative of the provinces.
AZMOODEH—the tried.
AZRAEL—the angel of death.

B

BAASENEE—the pipe of Chriſhnah the Hindoo Apollo—it is a muſical inſtrument, made with one perforated bamboo, ſimilar to our flageolet, except that each hole is not ſo exactly divided by notes, but many by half notes; its tone is ſoft and plaintive, and ſo eaſily filled that ſome blow it with their noſtrils.
BAAT—a claſs of bramins.
BABA—means father—but is given as a moſt honourable title.
BABBOGHAZY—the ſtrait's mouth—Babelmandel.
BAADCHAPPY—fees taken by the moteſib for affixing his ſeals to the weights.
BAADHATTA—the ſetting up of a haut or market near another, to its prejudice.
BAANS—very high and dangerous waves, made by the influx of ſpring-tides into the Ganges.
BABER—the name of an Indian emperor.

BABOO—lord—fir—mafter—worfhip.

BAB-E-SIKUNDUR—the ftraits of Alexander, which are Babelmandel.

BABUL MUNDIL, or BABELMANDIL—the lofty ftraits.

BABBOGHAZY—the ftrait's mouth—the fame place as Babelmandel.

BACTRUS—the name of a river—the fame as Gihon.

BADE, or AMBUSHT—a tribe formed from the production of a woman of the Bice caft having had connexion with a bramin.

BADJERA—a fmall grain.

BAGDAD—the gardens of king Dad—the name of a city.

BAGNAGUR—Hyderabad was formerly fo called—it is three hundred and feventy miles diftant from Delhi.

BAGUM SURRAD—a town about five cofs from Allahabad.

BAHAR—a province lying north-weft of Bengal, the inheritance of the prince of the empire, and governed by the nizam of Bengal—a weight of four hundred and forty-five pounds at Mocha, five hundred and fixty pounds at Bencoolen, and from eight hundred and fourteen, to eight hundred and fixteen pounds at Beetlefukee.

BAHAR BANU—the blooming princefs.

BAHARIN—a province—that tract of land which lies between the gulfs of Perfia and Arabia.

BAHEERS—people employed for carrying baggage.

BAJEZET—the name of a Turkifh emperor—it means endued with excellence.

BAJEROW—a famous general of the Mahrattas or Ganims.

BATIRS, or BACTRIANS—inhabitants of Baktir or Bactria.

BACKY JAY—fee *Jogee.*

BALAGAUT—the upper Gauts or range of mountains—fo called to diftinguifh them from the Payen Gauts, the lower Gauts, or paffes.

BALADUSTU—extortions or clandeftine collections.

BALK—a kingdom originally dependant on the Perfian

empire, bounded by Korafaun to the weft, *Bukaria* or Bukhara on the north, and by Sigiftan or Sheeftaun to the fouth.

BALLABASHROW—a Mahratta ·officer, in the fervice of Gazooden Cawn, who murdered Allumgeer the Second.

BALLAJEE, or BALLAROW NANA—the prime minifter of the Jahoo Raja, and chief adminiftrator of all the Mahratta affairs.

BALLAROW or BALLA—the name of a prime minifter, Jahoo Raja—the title of Nana was adjoined to his name.

BAMBOO—a meafure of a gallon—eight hundred make a *coyan* at Bencoolen.

BAMBOO—a fpecies of cane—there are two forts diftinguifhed, as male and female, the firft being folid, the other hollow; they are both of great· ufe in forming temporary buildings, in making mats, or as fupporters by which men carry large burdens—moft of the furniture which comes from China is made with this cane.

BANC, or BANG—a herb which grows like hemp— its powers are fimilar to laudanum, but not fo potent: it is very much ufed by the natives of India with dreadful effects.

BANKSAULS—ftorehoufes for depofiting fhips' ftores in while the fhips are unlading and refitting.

BANPERUST—one who, after his fiftieth year of life, wholly renounces the world to pray.

BANDIKOOT—a very large fort of rat.

BANYAN—Hindoo merchants are fo called in Bombay; they are of high caft—in Bengal there are perfons called Banyans who act as agents, for which they have about three pice in every rupee.

BANYAN—a garment worn next to the fkin.

BANYAN-TREE—is among the Hindoos a facred plant— from its various branches fhoots, exactly like roots, iffue, and growing till they reach the ground, fix themfelves and become mothers to a future progeny; they thus extend as far as the ground will admit;

there are two forts, the *pipler*, which is the female, the *ward*, the male: this is the fame tree which is called the ficus orientalis.

BAR—Saturday.

BARAAT—a draft or affignment.

BARAJEE—an account, ftating firft the fum total, then the particulars.

BARBEK—lord of audience.

BARELLY RUPEES—rupees coined at Barelly.

BARGA—the place of admittance, or the public divan where audience is given.

BARJAUT—forcing perfons to buy goods above the market price.

BARJEBEE, or BEREE—a tribe of Hindoos, produced by the connexion of a bramin with a woman of the Sooder caft.

BARRAN—rain.

BARRANNEE—a cloak as a defence againft rain.

BATOLEN—charity land allowed a clafs of bramins called *Baat*.

BATTA—an extraordinary allowance paid the military when on field duty.

BATTY—rice in the hufk.

BATWARRA—the partition or divifion of lands.

BAUBERIE—a kind of gourd—a noife.

BAUDGON—the fifth month—from the 11th of May to the 12th of June.

BAUDSHAH, or PAUDSHAH—a king.

BAUGH—a garden—generally with a houfe.

BAUGLEPOOR—a diftrict about 260 miles from Calcutta.

BAUHAUDER—a military title—fimilar to that of knight.

BAZAR—an eftablifhed market—whereas a temporary one is called a haut.

BAZEE AFTEE CHOKERA—lands appropriated for the payment of fervants.

BAZEE BABUL—the name of a tax.

BAZEE DUFFEE—the name of a tax.

BAZEE JUMMA—fines.

BAZEE JUMMA MATOUT—a tax, eftablifhed upon the province in general, in lieu of a revenue which arofe from arbitrary meafures, exerted over thofe who were guilty, or fuppofed guilty, of trifling crimes.

BAZEE ZEMEEN—charity lands—generally applied to land exempt from rent, by a grant from the emperor or fuperior of the diftrict.

BAZOUBUND—a bracelet.

BAZYAFT—refumed.

BEA—a river in the Jaut country.

BEÄS—the author of the heroic poem called Mahābāret—he fuppofes himfelf defcended from the Hindoo prophet Bifefly Mahamoonee.

BEASTIES—people who carry water in leathern veffels.

BEAT—the common thin cane.

BEAVRA—a forced contribution.

BEDAR BUHT—whofe fortune is awake.

BEDDINURE—the name of a country in the Decan.

BEDDOUINS—banditti of the defert.

BEEAKĔRUN—grammars in the Shanfcrit language—there are many.

BEEBEE—a lady—by the lower orders this word is frequently changed to *Boubon*.

BEEGA—about a third part of an acre; in the Hindooftan meafure it is twenty *quit-ha* or *bifwa*.

BEEJEE'SHUKTA—a public or common ball.

BEEKREEK—a man who voluntarily fells his own liberty.

BEEL—an inftrument like a large hoe.

BEELS—a people who live to the northward of Surat—they are a favage race, and frequently live by plunder.

BEENA—a fpecies of long grafs.

BEERBOOM—a diftrict ninety miles diftant from Calcutta.

BEESHOOKERMA—an artift who is related to have formed all the weapons for the war which was maintained in the Suttee Jogue, between Dewta and Offoon (or the good and bad fpirits) for the fpace of one hundred years—he is faid to have invented the *Agneeafter* and the *fhet Aghnee*.

BEET—a fpecies of fickly grafs which has prickles on it.

BEETLE—fee *Betel*.

BEETLEFUKEE—the name of a place near Mocha from whence a great deal of coffee comes.

BEG—fir—lord—mafter.

BEGLERBEG—lord of lords.

BEGUM—princefs—a title given to every lady of rank.

BEHAR—the fpring—the name of a province.

BEHAUDER—a title—the invincible in war.

BEHAUDER SHAH—the invincible king.

BEHAWILLY—the partition of the natural produce of the harveft between the government and the cultivator.

BEHEERY—an aftringent drug.

BEHER-E-AKHZAR—the green fea—by Europeans called the Indian Ocean.

BEHER-AL-MUZZULLUM—the fea of darknefs—the Atlantic Ocean.

BEID—the moft ancient and venerable of the Gentoo fcriptures given by Brihma—there are four : the *Rug*, the *Huchur*, the *Sam*, and the *Atreburn* ; they are written in a kind of meafured profe of the Shanfcrit language called *Ringtee Chhund*.

BEJESHUKTA—a bull which is kept for the purpofe of driving cows to.

BEJINTY MAHAL—a department in which all dancing girls and muficians are included, and from whom a public revenue is collected.

BEIT—a diftich.

BEKREET—one who of his own accord fells his liberty and becomes a flave.

REKUT—a flave for a livelihood.

BELAA KEROH—a principal department in the houfehold expenfes of a nawaub.

BELINDA, or WEILLANDA, or WULLUNDEZ—a Dutchman.

BELUK—a fief in Perfian—being a tract of country which belongs to a fubject by gift, purchafe, or fucceffion, or which is held for military fervice.

BENARES—an ancient Hindoo city, the feat of fcience in Hindooftan—it is fituated on the Ganges; it formerly belonged to the nawaub of Oude; it is about 540 miles diftant from Calcutta.

BENGAL—an extenſive province in poſſeſſion of the
Engliſh Eaſt India Company: its capital, Calcutta, is
the ſeat of the firſt or ſupreme government of all the
Britiſh poſſeſſions in Aſia.

BENJAREES—merchants who ſupply camps, &c. with
grain—ſee *Brinjaries*.

BENYEMEENY—the ſon of the right—the perſon we call
Benjamin.

BEOFSARY—a travelling merchant or pedlar, who carries
his goods on bullocks:

BERAMY—one of the five ſuperior modes of marriage—
according to it, the father by entreaty obtains a bridegroom of diſtinction, and on that account makes magnificent nuptial preſents.

BERAR—the name of a province.

BERAYNT—a bramin's ſon who is a minor.

BERBAKRUT—a man who becomes a ſlave for the ſake
of a female ſervant.

BERCUNDASS, or BURKUNDAZEE—a ſoldier, or any one
uſing fire-arms—it is derived from the Perſian words
burks lightning, and *undachtun* to throw.

BEREESOCHERG—a conſecrated bull ſuffered to go looſe.

BERENGE AROOK—rice cleanſed without boiling.

BERHEMCHARRY—a man who has ſtudied divinity for
twelve years in the deſert, without ſeeing the face of
any other tribe except bramins having before aſſumed
the braminical thread.

BERMOOTER—land for the ſupport of bramins.

BEROOA—a pimp—theſe people always attend on dancing women.

BEROOR—a tribe of Hindoos which took their origin
from the connexion of a man of the Abheir caſt with
a woman of the Koofs.

BERREE—a tribe of Hindoos, to whom the raiſing the
paun or betel plant is allotted.

BERT or BERTEE—charitable grants of lands or money
amongſt the Hindoos in general.

BERTUK—a ſervant.

BERUKPOOR—the city of bleſſing—the name of a city.

BESTAD—a ſtorehouſe.

D

BETEL LEAF—an aromatic fhrub of the vine fpccies—
the leaf is fomething like the bean—it is called *paun*
by the natives; the fale of it forms a monopoly in
Madrafs, for the allowance of which the Company receives annually to the amount of fome thoufands of
pounds.

BETEL NUT—called fopary—grows on a tree fimilar
to the cocoa-nut; it is larger than the nutmeg, of a
round rather flatted form: the natives of India cut it
fmall and mix it with fine chunam, or lime made
with fhells; it is then rolled in the betel leaf, and eaten.
When a perfon gives thefe, it is the fame as giving an
affurance of protection while in his company.

BETTOUR—a frontier town of the Cora provinces, fituated on the fouth bank of the Ganges.

BHAKHA—the Hindowee verfification is fo called.

BHAUGULPOOR COTTON—a particular kind of cotton,
which makes cloth of a nankeen colour without
dying.

BHEKUT—one who performs fervitude for his fubfiftence.

BHERTUK—wages—there are two kinds: one Arteh
Bherut, the other Bhook Bherut.

BHOOK BHERUT—is when a workman receives part of
the produce inftead of wages.

BHOOBUN—a fphere—the Hindoos fay, there are feven
below and fix above the earth, which fix are named
Bobur, Swergeh, Mahurr, Junneh, Tuppeh, Suttee; after
which comes our earth, which is named Bhoor.

BHOOK LABHEH—is when, inftead of intereft, a debtor
makes over any thing till the loan is repaid to his
creditor, who receives all the advantages.

BHOOR—the world we live on.

BHORTEKUNT—a name by which Hindooftan is called
in the Shanfcrit, from Bherrut, a name of one of the
firft Hindoo rajas, and khunt, which fignifies a conti-
nent or wide tract of land.

BHORTEKUNTEE—the name by which the inhabitants of
India were known before the introduction of the Tartar governments; they were alfo called Jumbodeepee.

BHUGUT—mendicants, monks, teachers.

BHYSE—the third of the four original tribes of the Hindoos—their duty is to cultivate the lands, to tend cattle; to buy and fell; for the Hindoos fay this caft was produced from the belly and thighs of *Brihma,* which manner of production fignifies nourifhment.

BIDDANOOR—the name of a country.

BIDGYGUR—a ftrong fort, fouth of the Ganges.

BIHISHTEE—divine.

BIHURJEE—A Mahratta vakeel, or agent.

BILDAR—a man who works with a beel—a pioneer.

BILDEAS—a religious fect.

BILKSERRIAS—fee *Buxerries.*

BINDARRA—part of the Mahratta troops, made up of all the different tribes of India; they receive no pay, but give a certain monthly fum to the commander in chief, for permiffion to march and plunder under the fanction of his banners—although they are formidable in deftroying what comes in their way, they cannot openly oppofe an enemy.

BIPHE—Thurfday.

BIPUL—fixty-eight make one pul—a meafure of time, twenty-four of which are equal to a moment.

BIRJ BHAKHA—the dialect fpoken in the province of Agra.

BISHEST MAHAMOONEE—the moft wife—the name of a great writer and Hindoo prophet; he is faid to have lived in the Suttee Jogue, or firft age of the world, and from whom Beäs, the author of the Mahäbaret, boafted his defcent. Bifheft wrote a commentary on the Beids, which is looked upon as the moft orthodox.

BISHEN PREET—land appropriated to the worfhip of the deity Bifhen.

BISHEVÄNER—that innate warmth which invigorates all the world—the mouth-wide opening of the horfe, made ufe of in the facrifice of the Afhummeed Jug, is called by this name.

BISSOULY—a town in the Rohilla territories.

BISSWASSROW—fee *Bow Jee.*

BISWA—is bifwañfa—and twenty bifwa make one beegha.

BISWANSA—in land meafure twenty make one bifwa or kutha.

BOBUR—one of the fix fpheres above the earth; it is that immediate vault of the vifible heavens in which the fun, moon, and ftars are placed, according to the ideas of the Hindoos.

BOGUEWILLER—lands allotted in charity for the indigent.

BOODHEWAR, or BOODH—Wednefday

BOMAN—the fame with bramin.

BOOK BERUT—a man who ferves for his fubfiftence.

BOOK LABBAY—intereft produced by ufufruct on any articles pledged.

BOONDHELCUND—BOONDELCUND—a hilly country to the fouthward of Allahabad, well known for the diamond-mines of Hieragur and Bunnagur.

BOORA TOKRA—an account in which the putwarree inferts the jumma, the receipt on account of the revenue, &c and formed at the end of fix months, and from which a new kiftbundy is formed.

BORAH—a Mahomedan fhopkeeper.

BORAK—Mahomed's horfe, on which he is feigned to make his nocturnal journies to heaven.

BOSSINEA—collector of villages in Rumpoor.

BOUTAN—the name of a country—it is alfo called Tibet.

BOUND HEDGE—a broad, ftrong belt of planting, chiefly the bamboo and the prickly pear; moft of the forts and villages of India are furrounded with fuch a hedge, and the large forts frequently have one which includes a circuit of feveral miles, to form a place of refuge to the inhabitants of the adjoining country againft the incurfions of the enemy's horfe.

BOUNGA—the baggage, and all furniture, appertaining a camp.

BOW JEE—the title of Biffwaffrow, the fon of Balla Jee, and commander in chief of the Mahrattas' army.

BOYDWILLER—donations to thofe who poffefs the knowledge of phyfic.

BRAMA—the Deity in his creative capacity; or rather

the fecondary Deity, who is fuppofed to be the immediate creator of all things.

BRAMA DOYAN—fignifies the fhare of bramins; that is,
all the perquifites, allowances, duties, and other gifts,
that have been, or may be, appropriated for the maintenance of the bramins, or other religious people.

BRAMAN, or BRAMIN—is a derivative from Brama, and
fignifies a theologift or divine—this is the firft caft of
the four grand divifions of Gentoos, who are from
their birth of the priefthood tribe; they fhed no blood
on any account, and eat no flefh, becaufe they believe
in the tranfmigration of fouls; and even vegetables
which have been prepared by any other caft than their
own they cannot touch: they can only marry with
perfons of their own caft, becaufe all others are inferior: their natural duty, according to the *Veds*, is
peace, felf-reftraint, patience, rectitude, wifdom, and
learning; as they were produced from the mouth of
Brama, they are to pray, to read, to inftruct.

BRANOLTORO GROUNDS—charity grounds granted to
the priefts.

BREEHESPETWAR—Thurfday.

BREEGOO—one of the firft created beings, produced
from the mind of Brama.

BREHM—the fpirit of God; according to the Hindoos
it is abforbed in contemplation, is prefent in every
part of fpace, is omnifcient.

BRIHMA—the Hindoo creator and legiflator: he gave the
four *beids*—fee *Brama.*

BRINJAL—a fort of vegetable.

BRINJARA, or BRINJARIES—people who fupply the army
with neceffaries of all kinds—they generaily carry
the things on camels, elephants, horfes, &c. &c.:
when there is danger they are efcorted by a detachment
from the army. Brinjara is derived from *brinj*, rice,
and *ara*, bringing. Thefe people belong to no particular caft, or any particular part of Hindooftan; they
live in tents, and travel about the country; many of
them have large droves of cattle belonging to them.
they are governed by their own particular laws and

regulations; they come frequently to towns on the
fea-coaft with wheat, &c. and in exchange take away
fpices, cotton, and woollen cloths, but principally
falt, which they carry to the interior parts of the country; they are rarely molefted, even in war-time, except by being fometimes preffed into the fervice of an
army to carry baggage or provifions; but fo foon as
their fervices are no longer wanted they are paid and
difmiffed.

BUBHAR—juftice.

BUGEROW—a boat fomewhat like our pleafure-barges:
it draws from four to five feet water; fome have cabins
fourteen feet wide, and are proportionably long.

BUDOR NOVEESEE—the auditing of charges.

BUDZOISTS—the name of a fect in Japan, who take their
name from Budzo their founder: the fpirit of Bud-
zoifm is dreadful; it breathes nothing but penitence,
exceffive fear, and cruel feverity.

BUHADOOR ULEE—the warrior. of Ulee.

BUHR-I-HAZIJ—a kind of mixed verfe, chiefly compofed
of the epitrite feet, and thus confifts of an alternate
intermixture of iambics, trochaics, and fpondees,
from whofe varied combination and arrangement the
numerous fpecies in this clafs originate, moft of which
are employed by the poets of India in their lyric, ele-
giac, and other metrical compofitions: we may divide them into ten octameters, called moofummum,
and eleven hexameters called moofuddus, which have
from fixteen to twelve fyllables in every line or he-
miftich: there are alfo twenty-four irregular fpecies
introduced by the Perfians.

BUHR-I-BAJZ—the iambic meafure, which likewife ad-
mits of fpondees and trochaics, interfperfed in the
form of epitrite, choriambic, and perhaps dactyle feet.

BUHR-I-RUMUL—a fort of Hindooftanee verfe, which
is diverfified with other long and fhort feet, fo as to
form from their pofition twenty-one fpecies, fourteen
of which are octameters, and feven hexameters.

BUHR-I-MOONSURUH—the flowing verfe—is alfo a fort
of mixed choriambic meafure, which is ufed for va-

rious purpofes, though feldom introduced in the Hindoo poetry: there are eight fpecies of it.

BUHR-I-MOOZARN—an Hindooftanee metre of a mixed nature, having the fame number of fix original feet, which are varioufly difpofed into feven octameter and one hexameter fpecies of lyrical verfe, and thefe are all very familiar to the Rekhtu poets.

BUHR-I-MOOQTUZIB—a fort of verfe, of which there are but two fpecies, both of which are octameter.

BUHR-I-MOOJTUS—a fort of Hindoo verfe, of which there are fix moofummum fpecies.

BUHR-I-SUREEN—a Hindooftanee meafure, which has but two varieties of hexameter verfe, and feems not unlike what is called the anapæftic meafure.

BUHR-I-JUDEED—a fort of Hindoo verfe.

BUHR-I-QUREEB—a fort of Hindooftanee verfe.

BUHR-I-KUFEEF—an Hindooftanee meafure, fimilar to the light anapæftic metre.

BUHR-I-MOOSHAKIL—a fort of Hindooftanee verfe.

BUHR-I-MOOTUGARIB—heroic rhyme, in which are written moft of all the larger works in the Hindooftanee, whether on war, morality, or romance: there are nine fpecies of it; fix octameters and three hexameters.

BUHR-I-MOOTUDARIK—an Hindooftanee metre, of which there are feven varieties, four octameters, and three hexameters.

BUKSHY—paymafter to the troops, &c. and treafurer.

BULBUL—the name of a bird which is the nightingale of India; it is larger in Bengal than that of Braun, i. e. Perfia: in Bengal they are trained to fight.

BULLIND AKTER—of high ftars and great fortune.

BULNUL—a fifherman who keeps boats on the river.

BUNARUS—fee *Benares.*

BUNDAREY—magazines and other offices for the magiftrate—the treafury.

BUNDER—A port or place where duties are collected—a cuftom-houfe.

BUNDHOO—a bank or dam.

Bundobust—literally, tying and binding—the regulation of any affairs—the difcipline of the army—and generally ufed for the fettlement of the Bengal revenues.

Bunds—dams, or banks to fecure lands againft inundations from adjacent rivers.

Bungalow—a cottage or warehoufe—a thatched houfe with walls of mud or matting, or any temporary material—a detached room or building.

Bunga Mellora—the name of a tree which bears a white flower, tinged with yellow; in the inner furface it yields a very fragrant fmell.

Bur—a tree—fee *Banian-tree.*

Burawind—an eftimate.

Burdwan—a country about fifty miles from Calcutta.

Burguers—things much like our rafters.

Burma—fee *Brama.*

Burmutter—fee *Bermooter.*

Burhanpoor—the name of a city—the words fignify the city of a fign.

Burraly—a large Rohilla town.

Burrun—the peculiarity of each tribe.

Burrun Sunker—the general denomination of all tribes produced by the intermixture of two different tribes; thefe are moftly dealers in petty articles of retail trade.

Burrut—a religious foundation.

Butkara—a weight of ftone.

Buxbunder—the office of cuftoms at Hughly.

Buxerries—foot foldiers, whofe common arms are fwords and targets, or fpears: they are generally employed to efcort goods or treafure.

Buxy—fee *Bukfhy.*

Buzar—fee *Bazar*—a fort in the province of Bahar, remarkable for the action fought near it between the Company's troops and thofe of Sujah ul Dowlah, headed by himfelf.

Byana—earneft given on a bargain.

Byapoor, or Vyapoor—as pronounced by the Moguls—

is three hundred and fifty-feven meafured cofs from Delhi.

BYONOS—a certain trailing plant refembling a vine, which grows on the ifland of Mindano—when cut into fhort lengths and bruifed, it difcharges a white juice that anfwers all the purpofes of foap.

BYSAC—the fourth month, from the 11th of April to the 11th of May.

BYSE—a feal—that of Tippoo Sultaun was a cipher formed by the intermixture of the letters of the words Nubbee Maulik, which fignify, The prophet is mafter: it is qt

BYT—a verfe.

BYTLEHEM—the houfe of Lehem—the city of Beth-lehem.

C

CAABA—the temple of Mecca.

CABEE CHHUND—in Shanfcrit poetry is a line of eleven fyllables.

CABOOBAT—an engagement.

CABUL—the name of a province and town which is two hundred and fixty-fix meafured cofs from Delbi.

CADIANG—a fmall fpecies of bean, commonly ufed by the Dutch on fhipboard, by way of variety of food for the crew.

CADY—fee *Kady*.

CAFFEELAS—large companies of merchants who travel from the interior part of the country, having oxen for the tranfport of their goods.

CAHAWN, CAHAWUN, or CAOUN, pronounced *cown*—fixteen puns of cowries, equal to about eighteen pence Englifh money.

CAJAN—a mat formed with leaves; they are much ufed to cover houfes.

CALARRY, CALLAREE, or KHALLARY—a falt-work, commonly called falt-pans.

CALCUTTA—the chief prefidency of the Englifh Eaft India Company: it is in the province of Bengal on the river Hugely.

CALIN—a kind of metal finer than lead, but coarfer than tin; perhaps a mixture of both: it is ufed in China for covering the roofs of houfes, and the tea-boxes which come from thence are made of it.

CALLUM DAN—an inkftand—the enfign of the Vizárut.

CALSA SHEREEFA—an office in which all the king's accounts are paffed.

CAMA PARCE—a place near Shawjehanabad.

CAMAR MEHAL—places where arrack and fpirituous liquors are fold.

CAMBUKSH—the youngeft fon of Aurengzebe.

CAMGAR CAWN—zemindar of Mey, in the province of Bahar.

CAMROODEEN CAWN—vizeer to Mahmud Shaw.

CANATS—fcreens which furround the king's tents, forming a large fquare.

CANDAHAR—the name of a province fituated on the frontiers of Perfia and Hindooftan, now the capital of Gifni and refidence of Timur Shaw, three hundred and fifty-eight cofs from Delhi.

CANDARINES—ten make a mace in money and weight in China.

CANDEISH—the name of a province: it fignifies the land of nobles.

CANDY—a weight, equal to about five hundred and fixty pounds at Angengo. Bombay, and Onore; five hundred pounds at Bengal and Fort St. George; fix hundred pounds at Callicut and Tillicherry; at Surat twenty-one maunds, or feven hundred weight.

CANOGE—the name of a city, the ancient metropolis of Hindooftan.

CANONGOE, or CANONGOO—a perfon fent to furvey the diftricts granted to the Company; he is regifter of the

CAU

fuba or province, and holds his commiffion from the emperor—the word means a fpeaker in the law.

CAPAAS—Bengal cotton, in contradiction to that of Surat.

CARAVANSERA—houfes erected for the refort of travellers by Mahomedans; perfons are appointed to attend to provide fuch things as rice and water gratis.

CARCOON—an officer under the zemindar, and alfo in the offices of government, who keeps accounts of the collections.

CARNATIC—a country on the eaftern fide of the Indian peninfula; it forms one of the moft confiderable nawaubfhips dependent on the foubah of Decan; from its capital it is fometimes called the province of Arcot.

CARRET—is equal to one eighth of a penny—five and a quarter make a bafeer, and feven a comafhee, at Mocha, and in Arabia, &c.

CASH—ten make a candarine in China, and eighty a fanam at Fort St. George.

CAST—a tribe; there are four original ones among the Hindoos, the Bramin, the Chehteree, the Bice, the Sooder; each of thefe are divided into many: there is a fifth called the Burrun Sunker; below this are the Pariars or Chandalas. The followers of Mahomed have alfo four head cafts refiding in India.

CATHAY—the ancient name of China.

CATTY—a weight equal to nineteen ounces and three quarters; one hundred make a pecul in China.

CATWAL—a judge and executor of juftice in criminal caufes.

CAVEER—equal to twenty-feven fortieths of a penny: eighty make a Spanifh dollar in Arabia, or a Mocha dollar at Mocha, and forty a Spanifh dollar at Beetlefukee.

CAUFFER—a term of abufe; its meaning implies a worfhipper of more than one god. The followers of Mahomed rank the people of the world under two general names, one the above, the other Mufulmaun or worfhippers of one only god.

CAULINUDDY—a rivulet feven cofs eaft of Furrockabad.

E 2

CAULPY—a town on the bank of the Jumna, belonging to the Mahrattas; it is about fixty-five cofs from Allahabad.

CAULSA—the king—fee *Calfa Shereefa.*

CAURTIC—the tenth month : it commences the 11th of October and ends the 11th of November.

CAUSSIM, or COSSIM ALLY CAWN—a late nawaub of Bengal, firft raifed to the mufnud and afterwards expelled by the Englifh.

CAUZEE—fee *Cauzy.*

CAUZEE SUDDUR—fee *Sudur Cauzee.*

CAUZY, or KARZI—a Mahomedan judge.

CAUZY UL KAUZA, or CAUZY UL KEZAAT—judge of judges, or head judge. There is one at Moorfhedabad whofe deputies are eftablifhed in moft of the Bengal diftricts : the court of this judge, formerly held at Moorfhedabad, took cognizance of caufes concerning marriage contracts and fettlements, the divifion of inheritances, teftaments, &c. At prefent this judicial power is not exercifed, being abforbed by the dewanny or the fouzdary jurifdictions : the cauzy ul kezaat has now a feat in the nizamut adawlut, at Moorfhedabad; but the feparate authority of himfelf and his deputies feems confined to giving fetwas, celebrating Mahomedan marriages, and attefting with their feals all deeds of purchafe, mortgages, fettlements, and the like.

CAWELY—fees received by the polygar for watching and taking care of the crop.

CAWN, or KHAN—in Perfia, a prince or governor of a province; in Hindooftan is the loweft order of Mogul nobility—it is likewife a general appellation to diftinguifh the Patans; and given to every man of rank.

CAWNPOOR—a fmall town in the Cora province, near the weftern frontiers, fituated on the fouthern bank of the Ganges—it may be tranflated the feat of nobility.

CAZAI MUMALECK—an officer fomewhat fimilar to our lord high chancellor.   o

CAZINAMA, RAZINAMA—a deed of acquiefcence.

CHABOUTRA—a tribunal.

CHAITE—the third month, from the 11th of March to the 10th of April.

CHAKERAM ZEMEEN—lands appropriated to the maintenance of public fervants.

CHAKER—a fervant.

CHAKERAN—account of lands appropriated to the maintenance of fervants.

CHAKRA—a kind of difcus with a fharp edge, hurled in battle from the point of the fore-finger, for which there is a hole in the centre.

CHAKRAN JEMMY GROUND—ground allotted to the fervants who are employed in the bufinefs of the revenue, in lieu of wages.

CHALISTOON—a building fupported by forty pillars; from *chalis* forty, and *toon* a pillar. The palace in Patna, appropriated to the ufe of the Shawzata, has this number, and is on that account called by this name.

CHANDALA—fee *Kandalahs*.

CHANDNI CHOK—the name of a fquare bazar.

CHAN SUMAUN—the fteward's feal—the fteward of the Mogul.

CHARSOMBAY—Wednefday.

CHATER—fee *Chitree*.

CHATEREE—fee *Chehteree*.

CHAUNDPOOR—the name of a town.

CHAURKUB—an upper robe, never conferred but on princes of the royal family, the vizeer of the emperor, and ameer ul omra.

CHAWBUCK—a fort of lafh, ufed at the cutcherry court to flog delinquents—this word has the general fenfe of the Englifh word whip.

CHAWBUCKSWAUR—the floggers, or ufers of the whip.

CHAWKS—a kind of guards.

CHECKREES, or CHUCKRUMS—an imaginary coin, of the value of ten fanams.

CHEEKS—lattices.

CHEETRA RATH—amongft gandharos—the title of chief of the gandharos, or celeftial choirs.

CHEHTEREE—the fecond of the four grand cafts of the Hindoos; they are related to have proceeded from the

I

arms of Brama, which fignifies ftrength; it is their duty therefore to act the foldier and the governor.

CHELAS—favourite flaves, adopted by their mafters.

CHELA CORPS—are compofed of boys, who, being taken captives, are made Muffulmauns: they were in the fervice of Tippoo Sultaun.

CHELAT—an honorary drefs.

CHELLER CAR—the fecond or fmall crop, gathered in April and May.

CHENDAL—a mean tribe of Gentoos, which arofe from the connexion of a man of the Sooder with a woman of the Bramin caft; their duty is to feed dogs and affes: they are not to live in the town: they are executioners, and are to caft out the bodies of fuch as die without heirs.

CHERMAKAR—fhoemakers, or workers in leather—a tribe of Gentoos who are defcended from a man of the Abheir caft having had connexion with a woman of the Bice caft.

CHEYKS—a powerful people who have from time immemorial inhabited the banks of the Ganges.

CH,HEDAM—a kind of money: its value is twenty kouries; or it is a quarter of a pyfa.

CHICKERBERDESHEE—compound intereft.

CHILLAMBRUM—a famous pagoda.

CHIN KULY CAWN—the fword-drawing lord: it is pronounced chuckles cawn.

CHIT—a note.

CHITREE—an umbrella.

CHITTA—an account and particular defcription of the boundaries of land.

CHITTAGONG—a diftrict two hundred and eighty-five miles diftant from Calcutta.

CHOKEDAR—a watchman—alfo the officer of a guard.

CHOKEY—a guard or watch-houfe—alfo a place appointed in different parts of the country, for receiving the public cuftoms and duties upon all branches of foreign and inland trade, paffing through thefe diftricts, and not included in duftuck privileges—generally underftood to be a cuftom-houfe, fituated by the river fide, where all boats pay a toll.

CHOORAKUM—boring the ears of a perfon to be adopted.

CHOP—a fmall feal on which are engraved the name of the Mogul, and the year of the Hejira.

CHOPERBAZEE—a game of hazard, played with three oblong dice.

CHOPPER—an exprefs meffenger.

CHORA, and CHORRY—two forts of lafhes, ufed at the cutcherries to flog criminals.

CHOT, or CHOUT—a fourth part—the word is commonly ufed for the tribute of the fourth part of the revenues, which the Mahrattas claim from many governments in India: alfo the duty collected upon judicial decifions in the cutcherry courts of Hindooftan.

CHOUD HUREE—chief—head.

CHOULTRIES—places built for the accommodation of travellers.

CHOULTRY—an open houfe for all travellers : the fame as a Turkifh caravanfera. A bramin refides always in or near it, to keep it clean, and to furnifh travellers with water, &c. ; he is maintained by an endowment.

CHOUT—fee *Chot.*

CHOUTARY—a Bengal corruption of Chout.

CHOW—fix make a grain at Bombay.

CHOWDRAWY, properly CHOWDRAYET—the jurifdiction of a chowdry.

CHOWDRY—a landholder or farmer; properly he is above the zemindar in rank; but according to the prefent cuftom of Bengal, he is deemed the next to the zemindar—moft commonly ufed as the principal purveyor of the markets in towns or camps.

CHOWKE—a conftant daily market, or place of fale, in towns, for all articles of wearing apparel, and other articles of fecond hand.

CHUBDAR—a ftaff-bearer, who is always one of the afuary of a great man ; he proclaims the approach of vifitors, and, with a filver or gold ftaff in his hand, he precedes his mafter's palankeen, crying his praifes and titles to the world.

CHUCKLÀ—an affemblage of fmaller divifions of a province—the jurifdiction of a fouzdar, who receives the rents from the zemindars, and accounts for them with the government.

CHUCKLADA'R—the fuperior of a number of dedars.

CHUCKLADARY—a tax to defray the expenfes of the chuckladar.

CHUCKRE—a fmall carriage for burdens—a cart.

CHUNA GUR, or CHUNARGUR—a very ftrong fortrefs in the province of Oude, about feven cofs from Benares, fituated on an eminence on the fouth bank of the Ganges, which river it commands.

CHUNAM, or CHINAM—lime: and even when in the form of mortar it does not change its name: that which the natives mix with their betel is made with fhells.

CHUPRA—a place in the province of Bahar, about forty miles above Patna.

CHURR, or CHERR—ifland—or fand-bank.

CHUTBA—the genealogy of titles of kings, read from the pulpit on all public occafions of worfhip, among the Mahomedans, after the praife of their prophet.

CHUTE SELAMY—a fee, taken from the bridegroom on the morning after his nuptials, and paid to the cauzy.

CIRCAR—the government—it is fometimes ufed for the diftrict or province.

CHYT—the name of a month, which partly correfponds with our month of March.

COBALLA—a deed of fale.

COCHUCH—the fmall feal of the kingdom, in oppofition to the great one.

COEL—a town in the Jaut country, between two rivers.

COFFOLA—a weight: about three pennyweights and three quarters of a grain at Mocha.

COJA—an eunuch—an Armenian title.

COILASGUR—a hill-fort, called Kowlafgur and Kylafgur, the lock of Heaven.

COIN—it fometimes means a fmall grain or bead of gold, current in the country, whereof eight make one bafhey: it is called furk in Perfia, and ruttee in Bengal.

Coir—the hufk of the cocoa-nut; which being cleaned leaves nothing but fibres, that are made into rope, which is ufed as that of hemp, and in the dry feafon is little inferior.

Colar—a fortrefs in the Decan.

Collee jogue—fee *Kollee jogue*.

Colleries—a tribe of people, who live in the Madura and Tinnevelly countries, as their name in their own language expreffes: they are by profeffion thieves: their weapon is a pike eighteen feet long, with which they creep along the ground, and ufe it with great addrefs in ambufcades.

Comar lands—lands, which, having no native tenant, are cultivated by contract.

Comassee—equal to nine tenths of a penny: an hundred make a fequin, eleven and a quarter a larin, eighteen an abifs, fixty a dollar in Arabia, or a Spanifh dollar at Mocha.

Commercolly—is about three days journey from Coffimbuzar.

Compound—a term ufed to exprefs an enclofure immediately adjoining to a houfe.

Congue—an inftrument which proclaims the approach of danger among the Polligar diftricts, about the Mugley pafs into the Myfore country.

Conjepoor—the capital of a zemindary of the fame name, in the Rohilla country.

Connys—a meafure of ground, three hundred covids long: two hundred and fifty at Luckypoor.

Consamman, or Consummany—the houfehold, or department which generally includes every expenfe belonging to it.

Cooly—the lower order of people who act as porters or labourers.

Coorsee—the feat near the throne, appropriated to the regent.

Cootba—the form of public prayer ufed for the king, or harangue read by the mullas, on Fridavs, in the mofques, in which the reigning prince is mentioned and prayed for.

F

Cootub Cawn—one of the commanders in Coonjepoor.

Cora—a small province, situated between the rivers Jumna and Ganges, westward of Allahabad, and with that province ceded by the English—it is also the name of a principal town in the province.

Corge—twenty pieces of cloth, at Fort St. George.

Corocoro—a sort of vessel.

Cortee,au—interest, which, in times of calamity, the borrower voluntarily agrees to advance.

Coss, or Cose—a measure by which distances are computed in India: there are two sorts, the *jerebi* or measured, which is about four hundred English yards, and the *resmi* or computed, which is from two thousand to two thousand five hundred yards, according to the part of the country. In Bombay the word *cofs* is frequently used for an English mile.

Coss, or Khas—lands under the immediate superintendance of government, for want of farmers.

Cosseed—a messenger employed to carry dispatches from one part of the empire to another—an express.

Cossimbuzar—a district, one hundred and thirty miles distant from Calcutta—there is also a town of the same name, the meaning of which is the market of Coffim.

Cossum—see *Cushoon*.

Cothoal—a kind of notary public.

Cotta—a spacious building or warehouse, in which the goods of the Company lie until they are sorted and packed.

Covid, Cuvid, or Covit—a cubit—in general half a yard, though there are some twenty-seven and thirty-six inches each.

Coultie—a kind of grain.

Courd—a native of Courdistaun.

Courie—see *Kourie*.

Cowl—an agreement, or proposal, from a superior to an inferior—protection.

Cown—see *Cahawn*.

Cowry—a small shell, used in many parts of India as

4

money: eighty make one pun, and fifty or fixty puns make one rupee.

COYAU—a meafure, equal to eight hundred gallons at Bencoolen.

COZ—ten make a fhahee in Perfia.

CRID—a poniard carried by all the Mallayans: it is a foot and a half long, and the blade is ferpentine.

CROOR—the Perfian for cofs, which fee.

CROOR—one hundred lack of rupees.

CROORY, or KAROORY—an officer of the government, who, for a commiffion of two or three per cent. makes himfelf refponfible for the rents of a zemindary.

CUBBEZOT CUBZ—a receipt.

CUDDY—ufed in liquid meafure: equal to eighteen pounds at Mocha.

CULLUMDAUN—fee *Callum Dan*.

CULLUSTAUNS—fee *Kulluftauns*.

CULNA—a town's name.

CUMMAR DUSHRO—an office, where the account is kept of lands that pay in kind.

CUMMER KESHAY—fees taken by peons, when placed as guards over a perfon.

CUMMY BESHY DUR TURDY—an abftract account of the increafe of the jumma of each

CURNUM—a writer or accountant.

CURRUCPOOR GAUT—the ford where the Englifh troops croffed the Ganges, in the campaign of 1773, near Ramgaut.

CURRUMBAUS—a town on the fouth bank of the Ganges, and north of Furruckabad: the river is fordable here in the dry feafon.

CURRUMCHARRY—the head officer of a gong, or village, on the part of a zemindar.

CURRUMNASSA, or CARRAMNASSA—a fmall river, which divides the province of Bahar from the territories of the nawaub of Oude, fouth of the Ganges.

CURRY—a mixture, eaten by all the inhabitants of India.

CURUANG—a gum, which is gathered from a tree growing on the iſland of Mindano.
CUSSHOON—a legion or brigade, confiſting of about
three thouſand men, cavalry, artillery, and infantry.
CUSSORE, or KUSSER—an allowance upon the exchange
of rupees, in contradiſtinction to batta: batta is the
ſum deducted, and cuſſore the ſum added.
CUTCHA AMDAUNG—the groſs import—the payment
made by the zemindar of his rent, in the various ſorts
of rupees as they come up from his different pergunnas.
CUTCHERRY—a court of juſtice—alſo the office into
which the rents are delivered, or for the tranſaction of
any other public buſineſs.
CUTTAC—the capital.of the province of Orixa.
CUTTAR—a ſword—it properly ſignifies a ſort of dagger
worn by the Indians.
CUTWALL—an inferior officer of the police, whoſe buſineſs is to try and decide petty miſdemeanours—an
officer who ſuperintends the market—chief magiſtrate
of the city.
CYRY—a green fruit: it has an aromatic flavour.
CZAR—a king or monarch: comes from Kezur, which
alſo forms Cæſar.

D

DACCA—a diſtrict two hundred and fifty miles from
Calcutta—the name of a city, which is alſo called Je-
hangeernugur, or the city of Jehangur.
DACHELA—a receipt.
DACYS—women who are appointed to act as peace offi-
cers in all cafes where women are concerned.
DADNY—the money paid in advance to a merchant or
manufacturer, on account of a contract for goods.

DAIE—property which can be bequeathed or inherited.

DAIE BAG—fee *Daie.*

DAIROS—the title of the fovereigns of Japan: they were at the fame time kings and pontiffs of the nation; but, about the eleventh century, thefe princes divided the ftate into feveral governments, and the viceroys have at different times made themfelves independent.

DAM, or DAUM—an imaginary coin, the fortieth part of a rupee.

DAMAHAN—a game, played on the ifland of Mindano: it is played with glafs beads, flat on one fide and of various colours, on a chequer-board.

DAMASHAHY—compofition of debt.

DAMDARY—a branch of revenue, arifing from bird-catchers, players, and muficians.

DAMMER—a kind of pitch taken from a tree.

DAN—a religious ceremony, in which the bramins pronounce a certain charm or incantation over any thing, in the wifh of a happy futurity, and give it as a prefent to another perfon.

DANAPOOR—five cofs weft of Patna, on the fouth bank of the Ganges, where cantonments are erected for a divifion of the Englifh troops.

DANDEE—a waterman or rower.

DANOOS—evil fpirits, or fallen angels: the offspring of Danoo.

DAR—poffeffor; from the Perfian word *dafhtun,* to hold— at the end of a word it animates and changes the in- ftrument to the ufer.

DARA—in the ancient language of Perfia, fignifies a fo- vereign or king.

DARA SHE KOWTH—in pomp, like Darius.

DASERRA—ten days appropriated to particular religious ceremonies.

DASSURA POOJA—a religious ceremony, performed in the month of Affen.

DAUB, or DOOAB—the two rivers—an appellation by which is diftinguifhed all the country between the ri- vers Jumna and Ganges.

DAVR BUKSH—God's gift.

DAWKS—poftmen, ftationed at ftages ten miles diftant from one another, for the conveyance of letters.

DAYANAUPAKAT—a flave by long defcent.

DEBASHY—an officer over ten men.

DECAN—a country fo called from its pofition on the fouth—it is the ancient Dachanos of Arrian.

DECOYT—a robber.

DEE—the ancient limits of any village or parifh.

DEEDAR—a perfon appointed to arreft the harveft of the ryot, in order to fecure the revenue.

DEEDARY SALLAMY—a tax on the parifh of one rupee annually.

DEEGWAN—an eftablifhment of Chokedors.

DEEIB—one of the five fuperior modes of marriage : it is when the jugg is firft performed.

DEEP—the world : the Hindoos fuppofe there are feven above this, and fome beneath, each furrounded by the fummodar, or main ocean ; the names of thofe worlds fituated above this earth are, *Jumbo, Pulkoo, Shoolmelo, Hoofhud, Kerunchud, Shakud,* and *Poofkerud.*

DEERA—a low caft of Hindoos; in the Cocun country they are called Purwaries ; in Surat, Sourties.

DEEWAN—a collection of odes, elegies, and fhort poems, of various kinds, whofe couplets muft terminate fucceffively with the feveral letters of the alphabet, till the whole are extended.

DEESMOKY, or DEESMOOK—principal officer of government in a diftrict : the office is generally joined to that of the canongoe.

DEHAAT ISTIMRAR—villages held on a cuftomary rate of revenue.

DEIOOL—a mean tribe among the Hindoos.

DELLAWAY—the regent of Myfore during a minority.

DELHI, or DELLY—the capital of the empire of Hindooftaun ; it is fometimes called Shah Jehaunabad, or the refidence of Shah Jehaun.

DELOLL, or DALLAL—a broker, employed by the gomafta in his dealings with the country weavers.

DEMBALCH—the whole crop, including both the government and the farmers' fhares.

DERBAN, or DURWAUN—a porter, a doorkeeper.
DERHASTS—propofals.
DERHUMS—fmall pieces of money ufed in Perfia.
DEROGAH—a head officer.
DEROOBUST PERGUNNAS—whole or entire pergunnas, which depend on a fingle zemindar.
DEROON—a weight or meafure : it is four adhuks.
DERRESHCUST—lands wafted away by rivers.
DERRIA SHECUSTA—encroachments of a river.
DESHAHIG—the head inhabitants of a diftrict, holding certain privileges above the others.
DESIE—the head over more than one village.
DESMOK—a fuperior defie.
DESORDESHELERCHA—particular difburfements of the zemindar, diftinguifhed from his charges at the fudder, &c.
DESPONDY, or DESPONDA—a head tenant, or villager.
DETROY—a proteft, or public declaration againft improper proceedings of the Indian government.
DETTAJEE TOPPUL—a Mahratta chief, who took Lahore.
DEVA DOYAM—the fhare of goods or duties, which are all the perquifites, allowance, duties, and other gifts, which have been, or may be, appropriated for the ufe and maintenance of the pagodas, or churches.
DEVANAGERIE—a particular language.
DEURAS, or DEWULS—the places of worfhip of the Hindoos.
DEUTAS—beings which the Hindoos fuppofe to inhabit the fpace between the heavens and the earth, who are enemies to mankind.
DEW—property which it is lawful to alienate.
DEWAN CLUMPA—outward room for doing bufinefs.
DEWAN CANNA—the dewan's office or court—the eating room.
DEWAN KALSY—the accountant general of the king's revenue.
DEWANNY—the office of the refident at the durbar, who acts as collector of the revenues, receives the monthly payments from the zemindars, difburfes the ftated re-

venueś appropriated to the king or nawaub, and conducts moft things relating to the revenue.

DEWANNY ADAULUT—an inferior court.

DEWAUN—the fecond officer of a province, whofe bufinefs is to fuperintend the lands and collections—the receiver general of a province—the fteward of any man of rank.

DEWITTER—free lands, held in the names of Hindoo deities.

DEWRY LANDS—certain lands referved to the family of the rajah, at the rent they were rated in the cutcherry books.

DEWTA—good fpirits—that deity to whom prayers are offered by all.

DEWUL—an Hindoo temple, or place of worfhip : in Europe it is called a pagoda.

DHEIBER, or JULYÀ—a tribe of Hindoos, defcended from a man of the Koop and a woman of the Sooder caft having been connected : their duty is to catch fifh.

DHOOBE—the name of a clafs of bramins.

DIARBEKIR—the name of a city and province : it fignifies, the territory of Bekir.

DIENAR—the name of a coin.

DIEWNAGAR—or the language of angels—is the name given to the Shanfcrit character, now ufed in Upper Hindooftan—it is faid to be the fame original letter which was firft delivered to the people now called Hindoos, by Brihma; it is however now much corrupted.

DILLEER SING RAJA—vakeel of Gazooden Cawn.

DINAGEPOOR—a fubordinate factory of the Company's, in the Purnea country, fituated to the weftward of Moorfhedabad, and two hundred miles diftant from Calcutta.

DIU—an ifland, on the weftern fide of India, belonging to the Portuguefe : it is alfo called *Diul*, *Deebul*, and *Dewul.*

DIVAN—a council of the prince and his minifters.

DIVAN INCHA—the principal fecretary of ftate.

Dobeer—a minifter.

Dobie—a wafherman.

Dobunds—fpecial repairs of dikes, or additional embankments.

Dokan—a fhop.

Dokandar—a fhopkeeper.

Dol—a fort of pea: it is frequently fplit, and boiled with rice, which mixtu e is called kidgere.

Dolle Potta—the form of a leafe.

Dooab—fee *Daub.*

Doob—fine grafs.

Doola-baher—a tribe, which fprung from a woman of the Bice caft having had connexion with a man of the Teilkar caft.

Dooly—a kind of box, large enough for a perfon to lie at full length: it is fufpended from a bamboo, and carried on the fhoulders of four men: moft officers carry one to the field with them for the purpofe of travelling, and ufing as a bed. They are ufed to carry the fick and wounded.

Dooréas—dogkeepers.

Doot—an agent or hircarra.

Dorcas—ftriped muflins.

Dorymancum—a new tax.

Doss—flaves: there are fifteen forts of flavery, which are named, 1ft, *Gerhejat*; 2d, *Keerecut*; 3d, *Lubdehee*; 4th, *Dayavaapakut*; 5th, *Eanakal Behrut*; 6th, *Ahut*; 7th, *Mookhud*; 8th, *Joodheh Perraput*; 9th, *Punjeet*; 10th, *Opookut*; 11th, *Perberjabefhey;* 12th, *Gheerut*; 13th, *Bhekut*; 14th, *Berbakrut;* 15th, *Bekrut.*

Dote—all games at hazard.

Doubash—fee *Dubafh.*

Doulbundabust—a rent-roll, formed by the zemindar

Doul Potta—the rent-roll of a farm, in the books of the cutcherry, which is fubfcribed by the farmer before he receives his order of poffeffion, according to which he pays his rents.

Dowlat Afza—increafe of fortune.

Dowlatabad—the fame city with the ancient Tagara: it fignifies, the city of profperity.

DROGA, or DAROGA—an overfeer or fuperintendent.

DROGA COSS—fuperintendent of the houfehold.

DROOG—a fortified hill or rock.

DUAN—*prime minifter—vizier:* the revenues and expenfes of the provinces, under the court of Delhi,
are fubject to his examination : he manages the cuftoms, and takes poffeffion, for the emperor, of the
eftates of the feudatories who die.

DUBASH—is the fame on the coaft of Coromandel with
the *fircat* of Bengal, if confidered in the fenfe of a
fervant, but not as a government.

DUB-E-AKBER—the conftellation called the Great Bear.

DUB-E-ASGHER—the conftellation called the Little Bear.

DUCHNEH—certain fees paid the bramin for performing
worfhip for any perfon : fometimes a father gives his
daughter in marriage in lieu of fees.

DUFFADAR—a principal or head man, next under the
mirda, over a body of peons : he is alfo a fubordinate
officer in the fepoys.

DUFTER—a place where papers are kept.

DUFTERBUND—a man who takes care of the papers, &c.
in an office.

DUFTERCONNA—the exchequer, or office for keeping the
government's accounts.

DULAUN—an apartment in a Mahomedan houfe.

DUL JUMMA—a ftatement of revenue.

DUMMADA—a river.

DUMPARISH—affault; there are three diftinctions, ab-
korun, neefhungpat, and keheet derfhen.

DUND—the fame as gurry, is twenty-four minutes : fixty
make one day and night.

DUNDEEDAR—a weighman.

DURANNY—fee *Abdallies.*

DURBAR—the chamber of audience, or court of the
Mogul, or any governor.

DURBAUN, or DURWAUN—fee *Derban.*

DURBAR CRUTCH—expenfes of the court.

DURBUSTY AYMA—lands the grant of which expreffes
one or more entire villages.

DURGA—a fhrine.

Durkhaust—petition or requeft.

Duroga—an overfeer.

Dussera—a Hindoo feftival, at the end of the rainy feafon.

Dussutary—in impoft of ten per cent.

Dustaveez—a voucher.

Dusthana—a piece of armour worn upon the right hand.

Dustoorat—certain perquifites, or per centage, allowed the zemindar on his jumma of his lands—fee *Malli-conna*.

Dustore—a cuftomary allowance or fee.

Dustuck—a paffport, permit, or order, in the Englifh Company's affairs—it generally means the permit under their feal which exempts goods from the payment of duties.

Dutt—gifts not approved, or which may be taken back.

Dutta—things taken away, which may not be taken back.

Dwapaar Jogue—fucceeds the tirtah jogue, and is the third of the four æras, or periods, of Indian chronology: in this age half the human race became depraved; it continued one million fix hundred thoufand years: the life of man was then reduced to a thoufand years. (See *Halhed.*) Mr. Roger fays it continued eight hundred and fixty-four thoufand years; Mr. Bernier fays eight hundred and fixty-four thoufand years; and Col. Dow fays feventy-two thoufand years.

E

Ear Ossadar—a title fignifying the grateful friend.

Eaz o'Din—a title fignifying the glory of religion—fee *Azeezooden.*

Eblis—the arch fiend.

Eed—a Mahomedan feftival, of which there are two

in a year, *Eed ul Zoha,* and *Eed ul Feller*; at the former, goats are facrificed in commemoration of the angel Gabriel's meffage from heaven to fave Ifaac; or, according to the Mahomedan tradition, Abraham from being facrificed by his father, and of his fubfti- tuting a goat or ram in his ftead: the *Eed ul Feller* is at the breaking up of the faft, at the expiration of the Mahomedan lent.

EEDGA—the place where all the people affemble to prayers, on the two great annual feftivals of the Ma- homedans called the Eeds; it has fmall minarets, but no covering.

EENAKAL BERUT—a flave, whofe life has been faved in time of a famine.

EENDRA—a perfonification of the vifible heavens, or the power of the Almighty over the elements.

EETALROW—a Mahratta chief, who took Ally Gowher.

EHEWAL—an account of the names of the ryots, and the meafurement of their different fpots of land.

EH,T,HER—an umbrella.

EILDIRM—lightning.

EKRAHAUM—a general acknowledgment.

ELEPHANTA—an ifland very near to Bombay: it is fa- mous on account of the antiquity of a pagoda which is cut out of a rock, and many figures.

ELLAAK—a fee collected at the fouzdary cutcherries, from the government peons, as a furplus, which they, to indemnify themfelves, exact over and above their diet allowance, from the parties over whom they are placed as a guard. In fome diftricts it is a fee or due taken from the litigating parties in fuits, on account of the government—when it is collected at the fouzdary cutcherries it is the emolument of the head officer there.

ELLORE—a town famous for its pagodas.

ELWAR—Sunday.

EMARUT—a building.

EMAUMBARRY—expenfes incurred by the king or na- waub at his mofques in religious matters.

EMIR—fee *Ameer.*

ENAHUT—a fecond depofit of any thing in truft.

ENAM—a word which fignifies *gift*: it is now particularly ufed as that from a fuperior to an inferior.

ENAKAL BEHRUT—a flave who hath been fed, and had his life preferved by another during a famine.

ERADUT CAUN—a title, which fignifies the faithful lord.

ESSAWIL—a macebearer.

ETAYA—a large town and fortrefs on the north bank of the Jumna: it is about ninety cofs weft of Allahabad.

ETMAUM—a divifion of a province under the fuperintendence of an officer called etmaumdar.

ETMAUMDAR—a fuperintendent over a fmall divifion of a province called an etmaum; he collects, in general, the revenues due to the government from the pergunnas, turrofs, and dees included in his jurifdiction, and tranfmits them to his fuperior.

ETMAUM CUTCHERIES—places to receive the fums due from the collection of farms forming the etmaum.

EZARA—a farm of the revenues.

EZARDAR—a farmer or renter of land in the new diftricts.

F

FACKERAN—the chief magiftrate of a large diftrict called a chuckla.

FAKEER—an Hindoo caft of a religious order: there are a great variety of them: they are always in the character of perfons collecting alms, and are frequently known to fubject themfelves voluntarily to extreme torture, in the hopes of appeafing an offended deity. They are in general a worthlefs fet of villains, who, to obtain money from the credulous Hindoo, put on the appearance of religion, under the cloak of which they commit the greateft excefses.

FAKIAM—or new—the method of calculation ufed by the bramins in the Carnatic: it is fo called in oppofi- tion to the fiddantam, or ancient method eftablifhed at Benares, which the bramins allowed to be much more perfeƈt, and fay that theirs was derived from the north.

FANAM—the name of a fmall coin, which is made in filver or gold.

FATEHEH BUZURGWAR—an offering made to the priefts for the fouls of deceafed anceftors.

FATTAHA—a prefatory prayer ufed by Mahomedans : it is in general the firft chapter of the Koran.

FATTEHABAD—the name of a place, which fignifies the habitation of viƈtory.

FATTEPOOR—the place formerly called Sickry: it is about twelve cofs from Agra—the name fignifies the place of viƈtory.

FEELCONNA—the place where elephants are kept—from *feel*, an elephant; and *conna*, a room or apartment.

FEIZABAD—the town of munificence.

FERD—a paper containing a ftatement.

FERD HUCKEEHUT—a memorial.

FERD SEWAUL—a petition.

FERIAUDY—a plaintiff.

FERINGY—a Frank : the name the Portuguefe are known by in India.

FERUNGISTAUN—properly fignifies the country of the Portuguefe; but it is ufed to fignify Europe.

FIRANSEZ—a Frenchman.

FIRANSEZ MUMLIKET—the country of the French.

FIRMAUN—a royal commiffion, mandate, or allowance.

FOIJDAR—a commander or magiftrate—fee *Fouzdar*.

FLAMINGO—a thing on which Brihma is fuppofed to perform his journies.

FLUCE—ten make a danim, and one hundred a ma- mooda, at Buffora.

FOUZDAR—the head magiftrate of a large diftriƈt, who has charge of the police, and takes cognizance of all criminal matters; he colleƈts the revenues for government: the diſtrict under his juriſdiction is called chuckla—properly fouzdar ſignifies a commander of a body of forces.

FOUZDARY—the office of a fouzdar.

FRAZELLS—forty make a bahar at Beetlefukee, and fifteen a bahar at Mocha.

FRESHES—overflowings of rivers during the rainy ſeaſon.

FRINGY—ſee *Feringy.*

FULKER—a revenue accruing from fruit.

FURHUNG—a vocabulary—a dictionary.

FURRUCKABAD—a large fortified town in the Dooab, ſituated at a ſmall diſtance from the Ganges—it ſignifies the *auſpicious town.*

FURRUCKSEER—a title, ſignifying of auguſt diſpoſition.

FUSSELANNA—a fee received by the cauzy on the harveſt.

FUSSLY—the year uſed by the Hindoos in records.

FUSSUL—harveſt.

FUSSUL KERREEF—the latter end of the year, beginning at the month of Caurtic.

FUSSUL RUBBY—the firſt harveſt of the year.

FUTTIGUR—a fort: the name ſignifies the rock of victory.

FUTWA—the name of a place twelve miles below Patna.

G

GAITREE—a ſociety, ſuppoſed ſomewhat ſimilar to the maſonic inſtitution.

GALAXY—the name of a river: the name ſignifies the trailing of the ſtraw.

GALLIVATS—a ſort of ſmall veſſel uſed on the Malabar coaſt.

GANGES—the name of a river, which is one of the boundaries of the hither peninſula of India. It falls

2

into India from the Sewallic Mountains, and empties itfelf from various mouths into the Bay of Bengal.

GANIMS—fee *Mahrattas*.

GANSEE JICKAY—a confumption, or fpitting of blood, or phlegm.

GANTAS OF SOOLO—twenty-five make a pecul of rice, equal to one hundred catties of China.

GARDEE—a tribe inhabiting the provinces of Byapoor, &c. : they are efteemed good foot foldiers—it is a name fometimes given to fepoys.

GAROORA—a bird, on which the Hindoos fuppofe the god Vifhnou to ride: it is a large brown kite, with a white head. The bramins, at fome of the temples of Vifhnou, accuftom birds of this fpecies that may be in the neighbourhood, to come at ftated times to be fed, and call them by ftriking a brafs plate.

GAUM—the Hindooftanee for village.

GAUR—the ancient religion of Perfia.

GAURS—the people in Perfia who ufed to pay adoration to fire.

GAUT—an entrance into a country—the word is now ufed to exprefs the range of hills which run along the Malabar coaft of the hither peninfula of India.

GAUTBARRY—a tax on boats, collected at the gauts or paffes.

GAUT-WALLA—the keepers or inhabitants of the paffes.

GAUZE O'DIN—the champion of religion.

GAUZEPOOR—a town and pergunna, eaft of Benares, in the territories of the nawaub of Oude.

GAZ—a title, fignifying warrior.

GAZAL—fee *Ghazal*.

GAZNEVIDES—a dynafty of Perfian and Indian emperors.

GAZNITES—durannies or abdallies.

GAZOODEEN CAWN—vizier to Allumgeer the Second, and nephew to the great Nizam ul Moolk.

GEE—clarified butter: it is ufed by the natives, and has the advantage of keeping long.

GEERUS—a voluntary flave for a certain time.

GEETA—an ancient fhafter, written by Adha,e Doom.

GEHENNUM—hell.

GEMSHID—the fourth prince of the firſt dynaſty of Perſia; he agrees with the Sikunder zoo'l kurryn of ſome Arabian hiſtorians.

GENGHIZKHAN—the name of a prince, from whom the dynaſty of khans of Precop Tartary ſprings.

GENTOO IDOLATERS—the oldeſt known inhabitants of India: they are divided into four grand caſts—which are called the Bramins, the Chehteree, the Bhyſe, and the Sooder; beſides which there is the Wurrun Sunker: each of theſe has innumerable diviſions.

GERBUT—a fortified city, which is as much as two coſs in length, and in breadth not more than four.

GERHEJAT—a child, born to a maſter by a female ſlave.

GHAZEL—a love-ſong—or ſpecies of poem, the ſubjeſt of which is in general love and wine, interſperſed with moral ſentiments, and reflections on the virtues and vices of mankind: it ought never to be more than eighteen beits, nor leſs than five, according to D'Herbelot; if leſs than five it is called *Rabat*, if more, *Kaſſide*; but Baron Ravinſky ſays, that all poems of this ſort which exceed thirteeen beits, rank with the kaffide; and according to Meninſki, the gazel ought never to be more than eleven: every verſe in the ſame gazel muſt rhyme with the ſame letter: it is more irregular than the Greek and Latin ode, one verſe having often no apparent connexion, either with the foregoing or ſubſequent couplets.

GHEERUT—one who voluntarily gives himſelf as a ſlave to another for a ſtated time.

GHERMKAR—ſmiths—a tribe of Hindoos, produced from the connexion of a Sooder man with a Chehtree woman.

GHOLAM MOHUMUD—the ſlave of Mahomed.

GHURRY—ſee *Gurry*.

GIDORE—a purgunna ſituated in the province of Bahar.

GINJAULS, or GINGAULS—large muſkets, of great length, uſed with a reſt, employed in the defence of forts.

GODOWN—a warehouſe.

H

GOHUD—a diftrict on the hills fouth of the Ganges.

GOITEREE—a Gentoo incantation, which is taught the bramin at the time of invefting him with the braminical thread.

GOLADAR, or GOLDAR—a ftore-keeper, or ftorehoufe-keeper.

GOLANDAAZEE—an artillery-man.

GOLCONDA—a caftle in the province of Hyderabad, by which the whole province is chiefly diftinguifhed in Europe—it means the round rock.

GOMASTA—an agent, or factor, in Bengal: it is generally underftood to fignify thofe who are fent into the interior parts of the country to purchafe goods.

GONG—a village, in Perfian.

GONG WALLAS—militia: from gong, a village; and walla, a man.

GOOTTY—the country of India.

GOSAEEN—mendicants—monks—teachers.

GOUMTY—a river in the fuba of Oude: it rifes in the Rohilla country, and falls into the Ganges below Benares.

GOUROO—mendicants—monks—teachers.

GOUSAIN—the name of a certain fect of Hindoo fakeers.

GOWA—a witnefs.

GRAB—the name of a veffel; fome are three mafted.

GRAINS—two and a half make a voll at Bombay.

GRAM—a grain fomewhat of the tare kind; horfes are fed with it inftead of oats—in the Bengal language the fame word fignifies a village.

GRAM SERAM JAMONEE—the arrangement of land fervants for the bufinefs of the villages.

GREESHMA—the hot feafon.

GUDDA—a fmall fort on a hill.

GUDGE—a meafure, twenty-four inches long.

GUNDAL—four cowries.

GUNG—the Ganges river—it is alfo the name of a tribe of Hindoo aftronomers; they were produced by the connexion of a man of the Deiool and a woman of the Bice caft.

GUNGE—a granary, or market for grain.

GUNGE BEHER—boats annually prepared at Dacca for the nawaub's afuary.

GUNNA BEIGUM—the wife of Ghaziuldien Khaun, a man of confummate abilities and wickednefs, who has borne an active part in the modern tranfactions in Upper Hindooftan, 1798.

GUNNIES—coarfe canvafs for bags, &c.

GUR—a houfe.

GURRATY—cantonments feven cofs and a half from Calcutta.

GURRY—a divifion of time, comprehending twenty-four minutes—but the word, among Europeans, is gen - rally underftood to fignify an *hour*.

GURRIES—mud forts; fome of them are furrounded with ditches.

GUSHT—in Indian mufic, a quaver.

GUSHT SELAMY—a tax exacted by the cauzies when on a circuit through their diftricts; it was formerly a voluntary gift of the farmers, but fince arbitrarily eftablifhed as a due.

GUTCHANNY—the impofition of goods on the natives at an arbitrary price, or the rendering any one againft his will refponfible for the revenues of a fpot of land.

GUZ—fee *Gudge*.

GUZERAT—the name of a province belonging to the Mahrattas, on the weftern fide of India : it is famous for cotton, &c.

GUZERBAUN—an officer who collects the cuftoms at the ferries.

GWALIAR—the name of a province—alfo a fortrefs, fouth of the Jumna, twenty-eight cofs from Agra.

GYLONG—a prieft.

H

HACKERY—an Indian carriage or cart, drawn by oxen.

HADGEE—one who has performed the pilgrimage to Mecca, which every true Muffulmaun ought to do once during his life.

HAFEZ—the name of a poet; it fignifies the guardian protector.

HAFEZ RAMET CAWN—one of the Rohilla chiefs.

HAJET NUKBEHA—papers requiring to be compared or adjufted.

HAJET SEEA—revenues remitted from the diftrict, either in bills or fpecie, and ready to be brought to account.

HAJET TUVEES—requiring inveftigation or inquiry.

HAKEEKUT JUMMA—an account fpecifying the revenue in all its branches.

HAKEM, or HAKIM—the governor of a city—a judge—a king—alfo the government.

HAKIM WUCT—the magiftrate of the time.

HAKIN—the reigning power.

HALBUNJIN—an anticipation of the revenue, by bringing part of the next year's rents to the account of the prefent.

HALDARRE—a tax on marriage.

HALLACHORE—an outcaft from the Hindoo tribes; they are called in the Cocunie language *Maung*: they do any fort of bufinefs which is of the vileft kind.

HAMED, or HAMET—the praifer—extoller.

HANIFA—one of the four great doctors famous for expounding the Mahomedan law.

HANSE, or FLAMINGO—a thing on which Brihma is fuppofed to perform his journies.

HARAM—a feraglio—or Mahomedan woman's apartment—the zenana.

HARCARRAS—meffengers employed to carry letters, and on bufinefs of truft; they are commonly bramins well acquainted with the neighbouring countries; they are fent to gain intelligence, and are ufed as guides in the field.

HAROL—the officer who commands the vanguard of an army—and fometimes it fignifies the vanguard.

HARON—the proper name Aaron.

HASAN—good—upright.

HAT HUCKAKUT—an account, fpecifying the affel and aboab-jumma of the ryots, and the fettlement of the revenue to be collected during the courfe of the year.

HATSHANA—an officer appointed by the zemindar of a diftrict, to meafure and mark out the land that each ryot poffeffes, and to collect the rents where they are paid in kind.

HAVILDAUR—an officer among the fepoys of the rank of fergeant, and next to the jemidar.

HAVILLY LANDS—diftricts attached to, and in the vicinity of, the capital of a province—the meaning of havilly is an habitation.

HAUT—a market kept on ftated days.

HAWKIM—a chief.

HAZAREE—a commander of gun-men—hazar, literally, is a thoufand.

HAZERZAMINEE—bail for the appearance of any perfon.

HEBA—a gift.

HEEMAT—the cold feafon.

HEETO-PADES—amicable inftruction—are a feries of connected fables interfperfed with moral, prudential, and political maxims: this work is in fuch high efteem throughout the Eaft, that it has been tranflated into moft languages fpoken there. It did not efcape the notice of the emperor Akbar: attentive to every thing that could contribute to promote ufeful knowledge, he directed his vizier, *Abul Fazel*, to put it into a ftyle fuited to all capacities, and to illuftrate the obfcure paffages in it; which he accordingly did, and gave it the title of the Criterion of Wifdom: at length thefe fables made their way into Europe, and have fince been circulated there with additions and alterations, under the name of Pilpay, or Efop.

HEGEREE, or HEGIRA—the name of the year according to which the followers of Mahomed reckon their æra; it commences from the flight of Mahomed from Mecca to Medina, July 16th, A. D. 622.

HEJAM—a barber—this tribe of Hindoos sprung from the connexion of a man of the Chehtree caft with a woman of the Sooder caft.

HEJAMUT—the profeffion of a barber; which is not to drefs the hair, a cuftom not ufed in India, but to fhave, pare the nails, and cleanfe the ears,

HEMAGET—protection—countenance—fupport.

HEMAGUM—an emperor of India—the word fignifies auguft.

HERAT—the ancient capital of Korafawn.

HIND, INDE, or INDIA—includes the whole country between the Burampooter and the Indus rivers, and Cape Comorin: it is now inhabited by various people, but it is fuppofed was formerly entirely poffeffed by the Hindoos.

HINDOO—the fuppofed original inhabitants of the hither peninfula of India—the word fignifies a fwarthy man—fee *Gentoo Idolaters.*

HINDOOSTAUN—a particular part of India, but frequently ufed for the whole: it is derived from hindoo black, and ftaun, country: fome fuppofe it to be derived from *Hind,* a fuppofed fon of Ham the fon of Noah.

HIRCARRA—a meffenger—a guide—a footman.

HIRSUNS—ficcas of various years.

HISSADAR—a fharer or partner.

HISSOUBE—accounts.

HOLOFERNES—wifdom—a name.

HOMA—the facrifice of fire.

HONDEAAN, or HUNDYVEAAN—commiffion on bills of exchange.

HOOKAH—an Indian pipe for fmoking.

HOOKAHBURDAR—the perfon who takes care of the hookah.

HOOKUM—an order or command.

HOOKUMNAUMAH—inftructions.

4

Hooly—a Gentoo feftival.

Hoosun mutle—when a poem only rhymes alternately—the fecond couplet is fo called.

Houn—a gold coin of the Myfore country, value about four rupees.

Houris—nymphs of paradife.

Housbulhookum—a patent, or paper figned by the vizier.

Howa—Eve.

Howalay—a depofit of property in full confidence.

Howdah—the chair or feat which is fixed on an elephant; it will hold two or three people, and has a canopy over it.

Hubba—a grain.

Huc Shuffee—an inquiry, by the cauzee and muftees, who is the next neighbour.

Hughly Wacca—a newfpaper, or chronicle kept by the officers of the Moors government.

Hul al Wazeerut—the vizier's fees.

Hul al Nissa—the moft angelic of women.

Humdum Ghumgusar—a title, fignifying the grief-expelling companion.

Huroof—the alphabet.

Hurray—an aftringent drug.

Husb ul Hookum, or Hassab ul Hookum—a patent or order, under the feal of the vizier, with thefe initial words, which fignify, Always to command.

Husseyn—the brother of Haffan, the fon of Ali—moft upright—excellent: the death of thefe two brothers is now annually commemorated by a certain caft of Muffulmauns.

Hustabood—a rent-roll, either of a grand divifion, or of leffer diftricts—an imaginary computation, or arbitrary valuation, which the cuftom of the country has eftablifhed.

Huzzoor—the prefence: applied by way of eminence to the Mogul's court. According to polite ufage, it is now applied to the prefence of every nawaub, or great man.

Huzzoor Balla—the high prefence.

Huzzoor Noveez—a fecretary who refides at court, and keeps copies of all firmauns, records, or letters.

Hy—the performer of the journies of angels; fo called on account of his fwiftnefs: he is fuppofed an Arabian horfe.

Hyder—the Arabic for lion : a title often given to men of rank.

Hyder Alli—the ufurper of the kingdom of Myfore; he is known under the name of Hyder Naik: his fon Tippoo fucceeded him.

Hyderabad—fignifies the town of the lion: it is the capital of the nizam's dominions. It was formerly called *Badnagur*, and is about three hundred and feventy-one miles diftant from Delhi.

Hyder Cooly—the flave of the lion.

Hyphasis—a river in the peninfula; it is the utmoft limit of Alexander the Great's progrefs in India.

I, or J.

Jackendar—an afforter—a Company's officer who fixes the price on each piece of cloth in the cotta.

Jaffeer—the victorious.

Jaffeer—one of the imauns, to whofe opinion, in feveral points, the funaies themfelves pay the greateft regard.

Jaffeer Ally Cawn—the nizam, who fucceeded Suraja Dowla.

Jaffnapatam—the town of Ceylon—the port of Jaffeer.

Jagemhou—a town on the fouth bank of the Ganges, in the Cora province.

Jaggernaut—a Gentoo pagoda.

Jaghire—from the Perfian *jaa*, a place, and *gheriftun*, to take—an affignment of the revenues of a diftrict to a fervant or dependant of government, who is hence called a jaghirdar. Jaghires are either *mufhroot*, conditional, or *belafhurt*, unconditional: they are frequently allotted to perfons for their military fervices.

JAGHIRE ASHAM—lands granted for the fupport of troops.

JAGHIRE SIRBAR—the jaghire of the government of the nizam.

JAGHIRE ZAT—lands for private maintenance.

JAGHIRDAR—the holder of a jaghire.

JALEIK—a tribe which originally fprung from a man of the Magdeh caft and a woman of the Sooder.

JAMA—a gown—the drefs which eaftern nations wear.

JAMABANDI—a contract, according to which the farmers leafed their lands from the officers of nawaubs.

JAMY MISJID—the great mofque.

JANIBDAR—an advocate, or defender—alfo a partial perfon.

JANNOO JEE—a Mahratta prince, the fon of Raghoo, and lord of the country of Naugpoor.

JAR BA VAFA—the grateful friend.

JASOIN—a Perfian word, fignifying fire-arms.

JA TEE BERUN KUSHKER—doing injury to a bramin—one who fmells of wine, or garlic, or onions—a falfe friend—one who ftrikes another on the buttock.

JAT—fee *Zaat*.

JAUT—a tribe of Rajapootes; they are Hindoos who poffefs a large territory to the fouthward of the Jumna: they are governed by a raja, who is called Soorudge Maun.

JAYDAAD— a fund, or fource; hence applied to fignify the ability of any diftrict or province in refpect to its revenue.

JAZZIAH—a tribute formerly impofed by the Saracens on all Jews, Chriftians, and Pagans who would not become profelytes to Mahomedanifm.

IBRAHIM CAWN—of the Gardee tribe, commander of the artillery in the Mahratta army.

JEBUN—a tribe of Gentoos, defcended from a woman of

I

the Bice having had connexion with a man of the Dewol caft.

JEDJER—a petty zemindary—the jaghire of a prince.

JEE—a title of refpect, much ufed, as fir—mafter—worfhip.

JEE POTR—a ftatement and decree.

JEEL—a natural fheet of water.

JEET—the fifth month.

JEHAUN ARA—the ornament of the world—a name given.

JEHAUNDAR—the poffeffor of the world.

JEHAUN GEER—conqueror of the world—the name of an emperor of Delhi.

JEHAUN SHAW—king of the world—a king of Delhi.

JEHOULDAR—treafurer.

JELCORA—revenue arifing from a fifhery.

JELLASUR—a town fituated in the Dooab, in the Jaut territories.

JELLITGUR—a bookbinder.

JELOUDAR—belonging to the train or equipage.

JEMADE—the name of a month.

JEMIDAR—a black officer, who has the fame rank as a lieutenant of the Company's forces.

JENANA—fee *Zenana.*

JENAUB—a river, and city built on the river by Alexander the Great.

JENNUGUR—the houfe of Jennu.

JEREBANA—a taxation on inhabitants, for defraying the charges of meafurement.

JERUB—meafurement of land.

JERUMANA—mulct—fine—or penalty.

JESDAUN BUKSH—the gift of God.

JESSOOR—the name of a diftrict feventy miles diftant from Calcutta.

JETH—the name of a month, which partly coincides with our month of May.

JEYA JEE—the name of a Mahratta general.

JEWAER KHANNA—the jewel-office.

JEZIA—a poll-tax levied by the Mahomedans on all other religions.

4

IHTIMAMDAR—a perfon appointed by the Hindoo magiftrate who has the fuperintending agency over feveral towns.

IJELAS—the general affembly of the court of juftice in Bengal.

JILAL O'DIN—the aggrandizement of religion.

JITS—an Indian Rajapoot nation.

ILLIABAD, or ALLAHABAD—the town of God.

JINS—demons, who perform their journies on one of the deformed tazee horfes, called *wafba*.

IMAM, or IMAUN—a Mahomedan prieft, the governor of Mufkat.

IMAMBARY—illuminations at the feftival of Mohurrum, where the fhrines of Imam, Huan, and Hoofaine are reprefented.

IMAUME—the name of a coin.

INDOSTAN—fee *Hindooftaun*.

INDUS—the name of a river which bounds India to the N. W.; it is one of thofe accounted facred by the Hindoos.

INGREZ—the Englifh: they are frequently called *Wullayet*, the country.

JOAR—a general maffacre of the women and children, which is fometimes performed by the Hindoos, when they find they cannot prevent the enemy from taking the town : a place is filled with wood, ftraw, oil, &c. where the victims are enclofed, and it is fet on fire.

JOARE—a grain, fmaller than the pea.

JOGEE, or SYNASSES—fects of fakeers, or religious mendicants.

JOGUE—the term for the different æras of the Hindoos : they reckon four, the futtee jogue, the tirtah jogue, the dwapaar jogue, and the collee jogue.

JOODAY PERRAPUT—a flave taken in war.

JOOJUN—about four cofs.

JOOLDAR—a cultivator, or hufbandman.

JOOMAN—Friday.

JOOTESE—the book of Gentoo aftronomy.

JOOZ—a fyllable, every moveable, or continuous letter

with a diacritical point, whether this coalefces with the next vowel or not.

JOULIE—a mat made with a fingle leaf of the cocoa-nut tree.

IRAN—Perfia.

ISLAM—means city; but is generally ufed as fignifying the true faith among the Mahomedans.

ISRUM—orders of men—or modes of life among the Hindoos, of which there are four: a berhemcharry, a finaffee, a ban peruft, and a koufholder.

ISTAUD—in Indian mufic, means flow.

ISTEMRAR—a rent not liable to alteration.

ITMAMDAR—a fuperintendent, or lieutenant-governor.

JUBUL-UL-KUSHUSH—the Turkifh for Mount Athos.

JUBUL-SOOS—the mountain of Sufa—Mount Atlas.

JUGG—a facrifice which is celebrated by pitching a tent on a felect fpot of ground, and making a fire there; ghee is then poured on the fire, and prayers are at the fame time offered to their deities.

JUGGUT GROW—a title given by the Hindoos to Akbar: it fignifies, *guardian of mankind.*

JULYA—fee *Dheiber.*

JUMBAUN—in Indian mufic, *fhake.*

JUMBOO DEEP—the world: it is a Shanfcrit word, and particularly fignifies India: it is derived from *jumboo* or *jumbook,* a jackal, and *deep,* any large portion of land furrounded by the fea.

JUMBOO DEEPEE—a name by which the inhabitants of India were known before the introduction of the Tartar governments; they were alfo called Bhertekhuntee.

JUMMA—valuation—aggregate—rental.

JUMMA ABOAB—the rent of land, fixed at a fubfequent period to the time of Akbar.

JUMMA ASSEL—the original rent of land.

JUMMABUNDY—rent-roll.

JUMMA DEHAUTY—the nett eftimated amount of the revenue of the whole dee or turruff.

JUMMA KERCH—an account, ftating the receipt and expenditure of the revenue.

JUMMA MOFUSSUL, or HUSTABOOD—the aggregate

amount of the different fources of revenue, whether rent or cuftom.

JUMMA PERGUNNATTY—the nett eftimate amount of the revenue at the pergunna cutcherry.

JUMMA SAYER—eftimated amount of lands.

JUMMA SUDDER—the affeffments demanded by government from the feveral landholders.

JUMMA WASSEL BAKY—an account of the rental, collections, and balances of any diftrict or province.

JUMMA ZEMINDARY—the nett eftimated amount of the revenue of the zemindary.

JUMNAH—the name of a river: it paffes the cities of Agra and Delhi, and falls into the Ganges at Allahabad.

JUNCAN—a toll or duty on every thing that paffes.

JUNGLE—a wood—wild country—ground which lies fallow more than four years—high grafs, or reeds—a thicket.

JUNGLEBOORY—clearing of jungles.

JUNGLEBOORY TALOOKA—a fpot of ground brought into cultivation by the poffeffor.

JUNNEH—according to the Hindoos, is the fourth of the fix fpheres fituated above the earth, to which the fouls of pious and moral men go: beyond which they do not pafs, unlefs they have fome uncommon merits and qualifications.

IZARA—fee *Ezara.*

IZARDAR—fee *Ezardar.*

K

KADY—a Mahomedan officer of juftice, who holds courts, in which are tried all difputes of property and all civil caufes.

KAFEEN—rhyme, which entirely depends on vocables more or lefs confonant with each other.

KAJEERS—a tribe of Turkomans.

KAK TOWDA—fine mould beat ftrongly in between two walls, for the purpofe of fhooting arrows into when the walls are taken away.

KALEE—an Hindoo deity, to whom human beings are facrificed.

KALALCONNA, or KALAULCONNA—a duty paid by fhop-keepers who retail fpirituous liquors; alfo the place where they are fold.

KALLA—forty, in dry meafure, make a *tomand* at Mocha.

KALLAAT, or KELAUT—a drefs given to any perfon in-vefted with a new office.

KALSA—fee *Caulfa*—the king—the head.

KALSA CUTCHERRY—the room of bufinefs, where the king himfelf fits.

KALSA SHEREEFA—fee *Calfa Shereefa.*

KAM, or KUTCHA WASSEL—grofs collections.

KAMA DOOK—one of the names of the cow of plenty, which was produced when the Deity churned the ocean.

KAMAMDAURY—grofs receipts of the revenue before forting—the fame as cutcha amdaung.

KAMBUKSH—the giver of defires or wifhes.

KANAKAN—vaffals of the fultaun of Mindano who pof-fefs large eftates.

KANAUTS—walls of cloth, fuch as thofe of tents.

KANDAHAR—fee *Candahar.*

KANDAYRUB—one of the five fuperior modes of mar-riage among the Hindoos—it is when a man and wo-man exchange necklaces or ftrings of flowers, and both make agreement in fome fecret place.

KANGY MEHAL—places for proftitution.

KANDALAHS—outcafts—thofe of the Hindoos who have been turned out of their cafts : their condition is the loweft degradation of human nature ; no perfon of any caft will have the leaft communication with them : if one approaches a perfon of the Nayr caft, he may put

him to death with impunity: water and milk are confidered as defiled by their fhadow paffing over them.

KANNA SHUMARY—an arbitrary tax laid on the farmers
by the zemindar.

KANUM—lady.

KARCONNA—a workfhop, or laboratory.

KARIGE JUMMA—alienated from the rental—the term
expreffes free lands.

KAROON—an eaftern prince, fo immenfely rich, that
Sady fays the keys alone of his treafures were fufficient
to fill forty houfes : he feems to agree with the Crœfus
of Roman hiftory.

KAROORY—fee *Croory*.

KARRAZEE CUTCHERRY—an office eftablifhed for the
collection of old balances, to prevent their interfering
with the current books.

KARTY AU—a voluntary offer of increafe of intereft.

KAYAY, or KASEH—a mixture of tin and copper.

KASHEED—a term in Indian mufic which fignifies,
length, or continue the found.

KASSIDE—or elegy—is the name the ghazel affumes
when more than eighteen diftichs.

KATA—the name by which China is known.

KATBARRY—fee *Gautbarry*.

KATIK—a month which follows Koonar, and partly coincides with October.

KAU EE KAW—intereft paid yearly.

KAUFFER—infidel—one of the two names under which
the followers of Mahomed rank the people of the
world—the other term is Muffulmaun, or believer in
only one true God.

KAULAUBHAIJE—a meffage.

KAULLEKAU—intereft paid monthly.

KAYAPELUT—metempfychofis.

KAYAPREKASH—or collection of poems—a Shanfcrit
work faid to have been compofed by one Kiyat, in
the third age of the world.

KAYAPREWAESH—the metempfychofis.

KAYTA—the defcendant of a Chehtree woman, having
had connexion with a man of the Sooder caft.

KEEL—wafte land.

KEERAY—expenfes—charges.

KEEREEUT—a purchafed flave.

KEET—a city of the fecond fize.

KELLA—fee *Killa*.

KEREEF—one of the two feafons into which the year is divided : the other is called rubby.

KERIMCHARRY—an inferior officer under the zemindar, who collects from the villages, and keeps the accounts.

KERHOO NIMUK—foreign falt.

KEROOR—a fabulous bird.

KEHSH—a caft of Hindoos, produced from the connexion of a Bice woman and a man of Deiool.

KEHT JUBENE—i. e. the tribe of Patnee: it was produced from a woman of the Bice caft having had connexion with a man of the Rujuk caft.

KERRUM, or KOIT—one born from a connexion between a man of the Bice and a woman of the Sooder caft.

KERUI—a parifh or village.

KERZDAR—a debtor.

KERZKA—a creditor.

KEZANA—a public revenue.

KHALLARY—fee *Calarry*.

KHAN—a title given by the king of Delhi, for which it is fuppofed the perfon maintains two hundred and fifty horfe-foldiers, of which he is the commander for the king's fervice.

KHALEFA—a Kaliph.

KHANDEDELA—fee *Chandala*.

KHAN KHANAN—a title, which fignifies lord of lords.

KHATRY—the fecond of the four grand cafts into which the Hindoos are divided: according to the Veds, their natural duties are bravery, glory, rectitude, generofity, and princely conduct.

KHAJA—fir—lord—mafter.

KHELLAUT—a drefs of honour, prefented in Hindooftaun, by men of rank, to vifitors of diftinction, but it is generally in pieces, and not made up; the number of pieces and their quality are in proportion to the rank of the perfons to whom they are prefented : fometimes it is fent as a prefent.

Khoda—God.

Khoda Bukhish—the gift of God.

Khodadaud Sircar—Tippoo Sultaun, the fovereign of the kingdom of Myfore, who fell in defence of his capital, Serungputtun, when it was ftormed by the Englifh on May the 4th, 1799.

Kheel—wafte land which lies fallow for three or four years.

Kheet—a fortified city, which is four cofs in length and breadth, and not fo much as eight.

Kibla—the point to which Mahomedans turn their faces when they pray.

Kjeu—a bridge through which the water paffes.

Killa—a caftle, or fort.

Killadar—the commandant of a fort.

Kinkobs—a fpecies of gold-wrought filk.

Kirk Pagodas—the name of a coin.

Kismis—a fmall light-coloured raifin without ftones.

Kismut—a divifion.

Kismut Purgunna—a part of a purgunna transferred from one zemindary to another.

Kisselbaches—foldiers.

Kist—the amount of a ftated payment.

Kistbundy—a contract or agreement for the acquittance of a debt by ftated payments.

Kistybundy—a monthly payment.

Kittar—fee *Cuttar*.

Kitubund—that couplet which fufpends the fenfe of one part of the fubfequent lines.

Kobir—great.

Kohistan—a province : it means the rocky or mountainous country.

Kojista akter—of happy ftars.

Koinbehkar—fee *Koombekhar*.

Koit, or **Kerram**—a caft of Hindoos, produced from a connexion between a man of the Bice and a woman of the Sooder caft.

Kollee Jogue—is the fourth of the four æras or periods

of Indian chronology: it is the prefent æra, in which all mankind are corrupted, or rather leffened; it is fuppofed to be ordained to fubfift four hundred thoufand years, of which near five thoufand are already expired, and the life of man, in that period, is limited to one hundred years. *Colonel Dow* fays, this age is to laft thirty-fix thoufand years: the age which preceded it is called the davapaar jogue.

KOMBAY—a large weight or meafure, twenty deroons.

KOODUP—a meafure or weight, about four puls or handfuls.

KOOLOO—the cocoa-tree.

KOOMBEKHAR—or potters : a caft of Hindoos, who took their origin from the connexion of a man of the Sooder caft with a woman of the Chehtree.

KOONAR—a month which partly coincides with September.

KOONCHY—a meafure of about eight handfuls.

KOONKORTEKEY GROUNDS—are grounds granted for the fupport of the families of perfons who have met with an untimely death.

KOONWUR—prince—highnefs.

KOOP—a tribe formed from the connexion of a man of the Bice and a woman of the Chehtree: it is their duty to take care of accompt-books.

KOOROOBA—a caft of Hindoos, produced from the connexion of a man of the Shoburun-beneik caft and a woman of the Bade caft.

KOOSIN—a fort of flowers ufed in dying.

KOOSOOMAKARA—the feafon of flowers, otherwife called vafant. The Hindoos divide the year into fix feafons, which are, feefar, the dewy feafon; heemant, the cold feafon; vafant, the mild; grefhma, the hot; varfa, the rainy; farat, the breaking up of the rains.

KOOTBA—fee *Cootba*.

KOPAULEE—a term in Indian mufic, which fignifies that the note is to be raifed an octave.

KOR—the fun, in the ancient language of Perfia.

KORD MAHAL—the leffer palace.

KOREISH—an Arabian tribe.

KOROPOSH—an allowance to zemindars for maintenance.
KOSE—a fpecies of herb, or grafs.
KOTE—a warehoufe.
KOTEB—the pole—the axis.
KOTEB UL DIN—the axis of religion.
KOTEB UL MOOLK—the axis of the empire.
KOTEDAR—a warehoufeman—an agent.
KOULIE—fee *Cooly.*
KOURIE—a fea fhell, ufed as money in many parts of
India: twenty make one ch,hedam.
KOYAL—a weighman.
KOYALEE—fees for weighing.
KRAMA—wooden fandals, ufed by the natives in the wet
feafon.
KREESHNA—an incarnation of the Deity.
KROOR—a million.
KUBBUR SELAMY—a confideration or due paid to the
zemindar by the Mahomedans, for his allowing them
to dig a grave for their deceafed relations.
KUDKASHTA—land cultivated by perfons who live on the
fpot—it alfo means the perfons themfelves.
KUFFEET—a fecurity.
KULB HUSUN—the dog of Hufun.
KULKEENA—a fub-leafe.
KULKEENADAR—an under-farmer of revenue.
KULLEAN—fmall quantities of land left uncultivated, for
the purpofe of laying grain upon it, at the time of
harveft, in order to its being thrafhed.
KULLUSTAUNS—Chriftians.
KULMA—the term for the Mahomedan creed.
KUMMER O DIN—the moon of religion.
KUNDEH-BENEIK—druggifts—a tribe compofed of per-
fons produced from a connexion between a bramin
and a woman of the Bice caft.
KUNDNEE—a fum of money annually paid by an inferior
governor to his fuperior.
KUNJUD—rape-feed.
KUNDHERPS—good fpirits, who perform their journies
on the horfe called Tajee.
KUNKAR—artificers in kafeh, brafs, and copper, &c.—

a caſt of the Hindoos which took its riſe from the deſcendants of a Bice woman having had connexion with a bramin.

KUREELUP—a ſmall vegetable of a bitter taſte.

KURIOF—ſee *Kereef.*

KURROL—the advanced guard of the main army.

KURUNLUK-DENZY—the ocean of gloom : the Turkiſh for the Atlantic Ocean.

KUSH BASH—perſons who enjoy lands rent-free, upon condition of ſerving government in a military capacity when called upon—the term alſo ſignifies people of middling circumſtances, who do not cultivate their lands themſelves, but hire ſervants to do it while they hold other employments.

KUSHEESH TOGHY—the Turkiſh for Mount Athos; meaning the mountain of monks.

KUTNA—fees on circumciſion.

KUTHA—twenty biſwanſa : and twenty kutha make one beegha.

KUTTEEB—a reader of prayers at a moſque.

KUTTRY—cloſets.

KUVVAUS—ſervants attending on the king's perſon.

KUZANA—a treaſury.

KWICKA—an account current of each farmer.

KYRAAT—charity.

L

LAAK—one hundred thouſand.

LACKERAGE—free lands that pay no revenue.

LACKERAGE-ZAMEEN—free lands which pay nothing to the revenue.

LADAVEE—a releaſe or acquittance from any demand.

LALA—lord—ſir—maſter—worſhip.

LAMA—a chief prieſt, whoſe followers ſuppoſe he never

dies, but that at his apparent death the fpirit enters the body of a new-born child : he is alfo monarch of Tibet.

LAMISSA—a female who officiates as prieft.

LAMISSA TUCEPAMO—or the great regeneratrefs ; her feat is on an ifland in the lake Paltoo, by the natives called Jumdro, or Jangoo.

LARIN—equal to ten drams and one eighth : eighty make a tomand in Arabia.

LASKARS—failors—the native gunners are alfo fo called— they are people fometimes attached to corps to pitch tents.

LATTIE—a warehoufe.

LAUK—one hundred thoufand.

LEEKUK—a fecretary or writer.

LEEWARIS—heirlefs—having or leaving no heir.

LESKAR—the camp of the great Mogul.

LIMBER—a two-wheel carriage, upon which the trail of the gun is fixed in travelling, and taken off when preparing for action : this gives the term unlimbering the guns.

LISSAN GHAIB—the language of myftery—an epithet given by many Mahomedans to the works of the poet Mahammed Shemfeddin, commonly known by the name of Hafez.

LOCMAN—Æfop.

LOOT—plunder—pillage.

LOOTIES—irregular horfemen who plunder and lay wafte the country, and harafs the enemy in their march.

LOOTYWALLA—fee Looties.

LOUTUF ALLAH—the favour of God.

LUBDEHEE—a flave found by accident.

LUNGER CONNA—an hofpital or poorhoufe.

LUT—a creeping tree.

LUTTA—the name of a large tree.

LUXHEBAR—Thurfday.

M

MAALER—a certificate attefted by the principal inhabitants of a place.

MAASIFER—a flower ufed in dying.

MAAZOUL—difmiffed from office.

MACE—ten make a tale in China.

MAETRASHY—cutting off the hair of a perfon to be adopted.

MAGDEH—fortune-tellers—a caft of Hindoos, produced from the defcendants of a man of the Bice having had connexion with a woman of the Chehtree : it is their duty to difplay the good qualities of the people.

MAGH—the eleventh month, which in fome meafure correfponds with January.

MAHABARAT—an ancient Indian heroic poem: the meafure of the chief part is in lines of eight fyllables.

MAHAGEN—a banker.

MAHA-PATUK—a murderer of a bramin—connexion with the wife of a bramin—whoever fteals eight afhrufees from a bramin—one who commits adultery with any of his father's wives, except his own mother —a bramin who drinks wine—or he who has been intimate with either of the above-mentioned for one year.

MAHAH RAJA—chief or great rajah, -

MAHA RANNY—great princefs.

MAHAJIN—a trader—fhopkeeper,

MAHAJAR—a banker.

MAHAL—literally, a place—any land, or public fund, producing a revenue to the government.

MAHALAAT—the plural of mahal.

MAHAL SERAI—the women's apartment—the zenana.

MAHARSHEES—great faints among the Hindoos: who reckon feven who were at the creation produced from the mind of Brama.

MAHASEBA—adjuftment of accounts.

Mahasebadar—an adjufter of accounts.

Mahalladar—an officer under the cutwall to prevent crimes and abufes.

Mahommed—praifed.

Mahommedan—a follower of the impoftor Mahommed.

Mahommed Shah—the celebrated king.

Mahurr—according to the Hindoos, is the third of the fix fpheres placed above the earth. Fakeers, and fuch as by dint of prayer have acquired an extraordinary degree of fanctity, go there.

Majua—a petty dealer or merchant.

Majun—a banker—or trader.

Makar—a fifh reprefented with a long fnout, fomething like the probofcis of an elephant.

Malabar Guns—fo called from being made in the Malabar country, are formed of bars of iron joined together : they are long, heavy, and unwieldy.

Malakar—fellers of flowers—a caft of Hindoos which arofe from the defcendants of a woman of the Bramin caft having had connexion with a man of the Chehtree.

Malary—judicial—belonging to a judge or magiftrate.

Malconna—a treafury—or ftorehoufe.

Maleeka—the queen.

Maleek ul Zumany—queen of the times.

Malguzary—rents—or land revenue.

Malik—the head or ruler.

Malliconna—perquifites allowed to the zemindar on the valuation of his lands.

Malwajib—revenues—or rents.

Malwajib Sircar—the government's rents.

Malzamin—a fecurity for a farmer of land.

Mamalukes—fignifies of the country—provincials.

Mamoodas—eighteen make a zingalee; nineteen and three quarters a zermaboob.

Mamooty—a tool to dig with.

Manes—the Perfian falfe prophet, and founder of the fect of Manicheans.

Mangan—a tax levied by officers of paffes.

Mangoo—the name of a tree which grows to a large

fize: it bears a fruit which has a flat oval ftone in the middle: there are various forts, fome of which are very fine.

MANJEE—the helmfman of a boat.

MANOOS—four beings produced at the creation from the mind of Brama.

MANTENIES—judges: there are fix in the ifland of Mindano, nominated by the fultaun.

MANZEL—ftages of the diftance of twenty-five or thirty miles.

MAR HAJAH NUNDCOMAR—the name of a bramin of the firft rank who was prime minifter to the nawaub of Bengal: he was tried, condemned, and hung by the fupreme council at Calcutta.

MARGA SEERSHA—a month which partly agrees with October.

MAROCHA HOLDARY—taxes on marriage.

MAROOTS—the winds.

MA'SHAY—of filver—is one tenth of a rupee of gold—one twelfth of an afhrofy.

MASHKAWAR—monthly accounts.

MASSOOLAS—a flight kind of boat ufed on the Corromandel coaft.

MATHOB—a taxafion above the original rent.

MATIM—death.

MATRANG—a term in Shanfcrit, which fignifies one whole tone: one matrang is a fhort vowel, two are a long vowel.

MAUG—the name of a month which in fome meafure agrees with our January and February.

MAUND, or MON—is a weight of forty zeer at Bengal; twelve at Madrafs; forty at Surat, &c.—twenty make one candy: this weight, according to the place, is different in name and weight,

MAUNG—fee *Hallachore.*

MAUZM—great—glorious.

MAUZ O DIN—the honour or glory of religion.

MAWANY—fee *Kiftbundy.*

MAYMANY—hofpitality.

MEANA—a vehicle fimilar to a palankeen, in carry-

I

rying one perfon, and being borne by four men, by means of a bamboo extended from the ends : it is generally feven feet long and three wide, with Venetian blinds, which flide and act as doors. Sometimes perfons will travel great diftances in them, when the number of bearers are increafed, and they by turns relieve each other: they will go at the rate of four miles in the hour.

MEEAN—lord—fir—mafter—worfhip.

MEERAN—dues—or rewards for fervices.

MEER TOZUK—a marfhal, whofe bufinefs it is to preferve order in a proceffion or line of march, and to report abfentees.

MEER BUKSHY—chief paymafter.

MEESURE—a weight; which varies according to the place.

MEGEMOUDUR—a clerk who checks the accounts of the aumil in each pergunna : his accounts are kept in the Mahratta language throughout the Carnatic; he is under the feriftadars.

MELABOO—a fpecies of leffer offence.

MELUXONE—an Hindoo deity.

MERHAU—a deduction—abatement.

MERKALL—a meafure equal to fix quarts: five make a para at Madrafs.

MERKARRY—dues or taxes levied at ferries.

MEROO—the north pole.

MIHTUR—prince.

MILANY—a comparifon or adjuftment.

MIM BASHY—a commander of one thoufand horfe.

MINAH—a bird, very common, which feeds on carrion.

MINNUT—the poetical name of Meer Quumeroodeen, born at Delhi : he is an acute, elegant, and animated poet.

MIRDAH—the head perfon.

MIRZA—fir—lord—mafter.

MISKAL—is thirty-fix rutta.

MISSUR—the title of a clafs of bramins.

MISTREE—the head man in any bufinefs, art, or profeffion—it however in fome places is only ufed for the head carpenter.

MOCCURARY—granted for life.

MODUCK—fellers of candy or confectionary—a tribe of Hindoos, who took their origin from a connexion between a man of the Chehtree and a woman of the Sooder caft.

MOFUSSUL—the country.

MOGUL—a caft of Mahomedans.

MOGUL OMRAS—thofe of Tartar and Perfian families, whom the Indians, without diftinction, call Moguls.

MOGULSTAN—a name given to India : properly, only to that part over which the Great Mogul is emperor.

MOHOOREE—a writer, or inferior clerk.

MOHUR—a gold coin, not always of the fame value, but in general about fifteen or fixteen rupees.

MOHURRUM—facred—confecrated—the name of the firft month in the Mahomedan calendar.

MOHUTERAN—lands given for the purpofes of religion.

MOHY-O'DIN—the revifer of religion.

MOJOODAT—ready money—cafh—fpecie—the unmeafured and undivided part of a pergunna which various perfons have a property in.

MOKASSA—a village held free from rent, on condition that the polygar will protect the property of paffengers.

MOLLA—a doctor of the law.

MALLAVIES—fee Molla.

MOLUGEE—a maker of falt.

MONSASIB—an officer who has the direction of the felling fpirituous liquors and intoxicating drugs; alfo the cognizance of drunkennefs—he is examiner of weights and meafures.

MONSOONS—that part of the year when the rains fall.

MOOBAREC OOLLAH—bleffed of God

MOOBAREC UL DOWLA—bleffed of fortune.

MOODY—a fhopkeeper—a grain-merchant or market.

MOOKHUD—a debtor who has given himfelf up as a flave to his creditor.

MOOLSERRY—the name of a tree.

MOODO—the chief of the iflands of Aiou Baba and others.

MOOKHUMMUS—when a ftanza of five verfes, or a tetraftic, is accompanied with a chorus, or returning line.

MOOKREE—or negative—a kind of epigram, written only in the Birj Bakha: it confifts of four lines, the three firft applied apparently to the tender fcenes of love; but on a queftion being explained which commences the fourth line, the point which concludes it is applicable to fome different fubject, the anfwers to this fubject always denying the impreffed idea.

MOONG—a grain very fimilar to peas, but black.

MOONSHY—a teacher of a language.

MOORRUBBU—a tetraftic of any kind.

MOORS—the followers of Mahomed, who are in India fo called.

MOOSTUZAD—where lines have a few words added to them, as in much of Dean Swift's verfe.

MOOSUMMUM—a ftanza of eight lines, has often three rhyming couplets, followed by one generally borrowed from another author, but with a different ending, and fometimes in a foreign language.

MOOTECOPHIL—an officer who examines accounts and puts his feal on them, when paffed in the fubordinate cutcherries, before they are fent to court.

MOOTIANA—foldiers employed for the collection of the revenue.

MOPLARS—a fet of Mahomedans from Arabia, who have eftablifhed themfelves by infinuation on the Malabar coaft, and have, by degrees, got into their hands the whole of the commerce, by which, and fupplying the Nair princes and nobles with money, they are become powerful and wealthy.

MORAUD—wifhed for—defired.

MORAUD BUKSH—the giver of defires.

MORAUD CAWN—object of defire.

MORUK—fee *Mourda*.

MOSHAIRA—perfonal allowance to zemindars.

MOSQUE—a Mahomedan place of worfhip.

MOTHIR AL MOOLUC—barricadoes—intrenchment—or breaftworks.

MOTUSUDDIE—fee *Mutfeddy*.
MOTUHURRIK—continuous.
MOULTASEDDIES—fee *Mutfeddy*.
MOULUWEE—a doctor.
MOURDA—a thing ufed as a footftool by Europeans, but by the natives as a feat: they are of different fizes, generally made with cane, and frequently covered with rich cloths.
MOWAKIL—a principal—or conftituent.
MOWROOS—hereditary.
MOWROOSEE—the ftate of being hereditary.
MOYEN ZABICK—a lift of febbendy and fervants employed by government.
MOYEN OOD DEEN—defender of the faith.
MOZCOORY—independent talookdars, who pay their own rents to government.
MUCHILKA—an agreement—an obligatory bond: generally taken from inferiors by an act of compulfion.
MUCHLIDAR—bearing the impreffion of a fift.
MUCHLOOT—land intermixed, belonging to one or more partners.
MUCKADUM—the head perfon.
MUCKATIL—a qualified flave.
MUCKREEM—an appraifer of goods.
MUCKUDDUMA—a caufe—or affair.
MUDARKAR—the principal of affairs.
MUDDUTMAUSH—a grant of land for fubfiftence.
MUDHOOR—the land produce, as diftinguifhed from the falt, in the latter diftrict of Bengal.
MUFTY—an interpreter of the law.
MUGS—plunderers—an Indian nation.
MUHARAJ—prince—highnefs.
MUHRA—chief—head.
MUHTO—chief—head.
MULL—a tribe of Hindoos, who fprung from a woman of the Sooder caft having had connexion with a man of the Dheiber caft.
MULLA—a Mahomedan judge—an interpreter.
MULLI KA TAUNIE—a fpoon-meat which is often produced at fupper: it is made hot with fpices.

3

MULLICK OO TOOJAR—comptrollers of commerce.

MULLUKERRHEE—a tribe of Hindoos, produced from the connexion of the Sherrunkar and a woman of the Ambuſht caſt.

MULMULS—muſlins.

MULUK—a general term for Hindoo tribes who eat prohibited food: they are ſprung from the members of the tyrannic Bein.

MUNADDY—a ſmall drum that is beat about to give notice of any thing.

MUNDUL—a perſon choſen from among the oldeſt inhabitants of a village to regulate their crops, and accommodate petty differences.

MUNEE HURRENEH CHHUND—in Shanſcrit poetry, ſignifies a line of twelve or nineteen ſyllables, which is ſcanned by three ſyllables in a foot; and the moſt approved foot is the anapæſt.

MUNGULWAR—Tueſday.

MUNGOSS—a large kind of rat.

MUNNET—a promiſe to pay a ſum of money: in which promiſe confidence, as in a writing, may be placed.

MUNNŒGAR—the head peon.

MUNNYCAWELY—taxes levied by the zemindars for the protection of a diſtrict.

MUNSEF—a judge—or juſtice.

MUNSOOR, or MUNSUR CAWN—victorious lord.

MUNSUB—a title, which gives the holder the right to be commander of ſeven thouſand horſe.

MUNSUBDARS—perſons inveſted with dignities.

MUNTUR—a text of the Shaſter.

MUQTU—a ſort of verſe, which preſerves only a very childiſh conceit by expreſſing the author's agnomen, here termed tukhulloos.

MURSEEN—elegy.

MURSHEDABAD—the city of inſtructors.

MURZAFAJING—the invincible.

MUSCOORAUT—ſundry articles of charges not included in the houſehold charges.

MUSHRIF—an officer of the treaſury to authenticate accounts and writings.

Musnud—a feat—but it particularly expreſſes the throne of a prince.

Musseed—a Mahomedan place of worſhip.

Mussuk—a ſkin in which water is carried: it is as much as one man can bear over the ſhoulders.

Mustapha—the elect.

Mustophy—examiner of accounts—the principal officer in the department wherein the accounts of diſmiſſed aumils are examined.

Mutahed—the fame as Wadadar.

Mutariffa—a duty on tea, paid by people of particular occupations.

Mut haaheds—people employed in the collection of the revenues under certain regulations.

Mut Hooter—a denial.

Mutlu—the opening diſtich of a poem: it is commonly in rhyme, though the ſubſequent lines are ſo only alternately.

Mutseddy, properly Motusuddie—an officer of ſtate, or collector of cuſtoms—a term applied to the officers employed in taking the accounts of the ſuba.

Mutsingwood—the ſuperintendent of polity on the iſland of Mindano.

Muttulluck Vakeel—an agent with full powers.

Muxadabad, properly Muxsoodabad—the town of one's choice.

N

Nabob, properly Nawaub—the plural of naib—a title given to every perſon of noble rank—the governor of a province is ſo called—in the regiſters of the throne of Delhi it is ſynonymous with ſoubahdar.

Naccal—a regiſter of all the leafes.

Nachine—a ſmall grain of the Myſore.

NADIR—wonderful.

NADIR SHAH—the wonderful king.

NADIR COOLY—the flave of God.

NAGAADS—winders of raw filk.

NAGARA—the drum made from a hollow cylinder of teek wood, and the ends covered with goat fkin : it is fufpended from the left fhoulder to the right fide, and beat with a ftick made of teek wood.

NAGGUR—the principal drum in Afiatic armies, commonly allowed to perfons of high dignity.

NAGUREE, or HINDUWEE—a writing character ufed in Bengal, &c. : it has thirty letters, and is that in which the Hindooftanee was written, before the Mahomedans introduced the Perfian character.

NAJALL—deficiency in produce.

NAIB—a deputy—the governor of a town under a nawaub.

NAIC, or NAIG—a fubaltern officer of the fepoys equal in rank to a corporal.

NAIRS—the nobility of the Malabar coaft : many affirm that they are the oldeft nobility in the world ; the ancient writers mention them, and quote the law which allows the Nair ladies to have many hufbands.

NAKARCONNA—the place where all the drums and war mufic are kept.

NAKOUDA—captain—or pilot.

NAKSHATRAS—difpellers of darknefs—the eighteen conftellations through which the moon paffes in her monthly courfe—conftellations in general.

NANA—the title of the king of the Mahrattas—or, properly, the acting head of the government, and general of the forces : the nominal head being ftyled Ram Raja and Saha Raja.

NANCAR—an allowance in an affignment upon the revenues, or the lands themfelves, originally given as charity for the relief of the poor.

NANCAR LANDS—part of the zemindary exempted from revenues, or fet apart for the immediate fupport of the zemindar.

NANDEE BUZURGWAR—the performance of the fateheh buzurgwar by the bridegroom before the marriage exhortation is pronounced.

NARAD—one of the devarfhees, and a great prophet, who is fuppofed to be ftill wandering about the world: *nara* fignifies a thread or clew, a precept; and *da*, a giver.

NAREKHA—the Hindoo name for the infernal regions, which are fuppofed to be divided into a variety of places adapted to different degrees of punifhment.

NARGHENNY WORSHIP—that of the invifible.

NAR O DIN—the fupporter of religion.

NASR JUNG—victorious in war.

NATT—dancers: a caft of Hindoos, which originally fprung from a man of the Malakar caft having had connexion with a woman of the Sooder.

NAUTCURNUM—hereditary village accountant.

NAUTWAN—a head tenant—or villager.

NAWAUB—fee *Nabob*.

NAZEM MUNAZEM—the placer in order.

NAZER—an overfeer ftationed at the kalfa, whofe bufinefs is to fend peons to enforce the payment of the revenues, to call aumils, or any officer of collections, to the cutcherry.

NAZERANNA—a fum paid to government, as an acknowledgment for a grant of lands, or any public office.

NAZERANNA—fubadary—fees of the vizier.

NAZERUT—the office of nazer.

NAZIM—the firft officer of a province, in whofe hands the executive power is lodged: ufually ftyled the nawaub.

NAZR—prefented to view—a term from an inferior to a fuperior.

NEABUT—a deputyfhip—or lieutenancy : from naib.

NEAMUT—a tax levied from the zemindar by the farmers.

NEASH—a depofit to prevent a feizure of effects.

NECAS NOVEEZ—an officer in the zeminday cutcherry, who examines the accounts of the collections in the country.

NEEDEE—to find any article loft.

NEEJOOT—fuch lands as are cultivated by the zemindar himfelf, and are rent-free.

NEEKHEEP—a depofit in confidence.

NEEM ASTEEN—an upper robe with half-fleeves, commonly made of gold or filver tiffue.

NREMODAR—a compenfation given by the farmer for not afcertaining lands.

NEEM TACKEE—an allowance given by the zemindars to the canongoes, at the rate of eight annas per hundred rupees on the affel jumma.

NEEMTUK KERM—occafional worfhip for holydays, and the performance of the dan and of the feradeh, during the eclipfes of the fun and moon.

NEESHUNGPAT—a violent affault without bloodfhed.

NEETEE SASTRAS—fyftems of morality and policy.

NEGABAR—a guard.

NEJOOM—an aftrologer.

NERCH DROGA—a clerk of the market.

NERMA—a kind of cotton which is perennial.

NESH ALLAH—affifted by God.

NESHAUNBURDAR—an enfign.

NEZZER—fee *Nazr*.

NIGHER—any fortified city, of at leaft eight cofs in length and breadth.

NIQUIBS—officers fimilar to corporals.

NIRENJ—a teller of tales—or reciter of hiftories.

NISHAUN—a letter of a prince.

NISSICKSHY BASHY—head regulator—or manager.

NIZAM—an orderer—adjufter—arranger—a title, beftowed by the Great Mogul on one of his principal viziers, upon his being invefted with the adminiftration of certain provinces.

NIZAM UL MOOLUC—the protector of the country.

NIZAMUT—the office of nizam.

NIZAMUT LANDS—fuch lands as have always remained in the hands of the zemindar, without ever having been granted in jaghire.

NOBUT CONNA—the apartment where the nobut is beaten.

M

NOMADES—wandering Arabs.
NOROSE—the day on which the fun enters Aries.
NOVEESENDAR—a writer—or clerk.
NOUR JEHAUN—light of the world.
NOUR O DEEN—the light of religion.
NOWARRA—an eſtabliſhment of boats at Dacca, kept for a defence againſt the Mugs, &c.
NOWAZUSH—poſſeſſing ability.
NUDDEE—the name for a rivulet.
NUFFERS—hereditary ſlaves.
NUJOOMEE—a caſt of Hindoos whoſe duty it is to be employed with the jooteeſe or ſhafter of aſtronomy.
NULLA—a rivulet—although there is no water, the place once a bed ſtill retains the ſame name.
NUNNEAS—people who work at the faltpetre in Bengal.
NUSEHA—the office wherein the papers of the revenue, that were annually ſent to the emperor, were prepared.
NUSHAWN—a grant given, or paper ſigned by the ſon of the Great Mogul.
NUSR MOOQUFFA—poetical proſe: the very reverſe of our blank verſe: the Coran is moſtly written in this proſe—ſee *Alcoran*—it is much adopted in the introduction to epiſtolary correſpondence.
NUT KERM—daily worſhip, and works of piety.
NUZZUR—an offering expreſſive of ſubmiſſion.

O

ODADAR—an officer of the revenues.
OKEREE—a caſt of Hindoos which ſprung from the connexion of a man of the Chehtree caſt with a woman of the Sooder.
OMDAT—a pillar—prop—ſupport.

4

OMEDWAR—lands remaining to be leafed out.

OMRA—plural of ameer, a lord.

OOM—a myftic emblem of the Deity, which is forbidden to be pronounced but in filence: it is fuppofed to fignify the Deity, and to be compofed of Shanfcrit roots or letters, the firft of which ftands for creator, fecond, preferver, and the third, deftroyer: an analogy has been found between this monofyllable, and the Egyptian *On.*

OORAGAS—the things which crawl on their breafts, as ferpents.

OORDO DIALECT—the polifhed language of the court: which is a dialect much intermixed with the Arabic and Perfian.

OOSANA—the preceptor of evil fpirits.

OOSTA—mafter.

OPADHEE—a term which expreffes the vices: luft, anger, avarice, folly, drunkennefs, and pride.

OPOOKUT—a voluntary flave.

OPOO PATUK—a diffolute character.

ORMUZD—the genius of good among the ancient Perfians.

OSSOOR—bad fpirits.

OULA—a drug: ufed, when mixed with oil, for the hair.

OUTPUN—produce or rent-roll of a diftrict.

OUZUN—literally, weight—the word is ufed to fignify a tax upon the revenue actually collected: originally meant to compenfate for rupees of fhort weight.

P

PAAN—a leaf in which the betel-nut, with the other ingredients, are put and eaten.

PAAT—a promiffory note.

PAATWAN—an allowance of ten per cent.
PADDY—rice in the huſk, whether dry or green.
PADRE—a Chriſtian prieſt.
PADSHA—king.
PAGODA—the place of worſhip of the Hindoos—the name of a gold coin of the value of eight rupees.
PAISHCUSH—tribute.
PAK PARISH—falſe accuſation.
PALANKEEN—a vehicle carried on the ſhoulders of four men, by means of a bamboo pole extending from each end : it carries one perſon in a reclining poſture ; it has a canopy which is ſupported by a pole raiſed along the centre, from whence it is pendent on either ſide.
PALEAGAS—ſee *Polygars*.
PALKEE—ſee *Palankeen*.
PANDAL—a temporary room.
PANDE—the title of a claſs of bramins.
PAPUAS—a people ſo called.
PARA—in meaſure, equal to five pecks, or thirty-four pounds eight ounces and twelve drams.
PARAGANA—ſee *Pergunna*.
PARHEZ BANU—the abſtinent princeſs.
PARIAH—a low caſt of Hindoos—any thing bad is termed pariah.
PARR—a diviſion of time, conſiſting of ſuch a number of gurries as will form nearly a fourth part of the natural day or night.
PARR GUNGE—a place where corn is ſold.
PARWARRY—a caſt of Hindoos.
PATAMAT—a two-maſt veſſel: each maſt carries one ſail of four unequal ſides—a meſſenger.
PATANS—a caſt of Mahomedans : they are generally known by Khan following their names.
PATCH—three pieces of cloth at Madraſs.
PAVAK—the god of fire.
PAVALUNGE—the name of a year.
PAUDSHAU—king.
PAUPAU—a fruit, in appearance and taſte ſomething like a melon: it grows on a ſmall tree which produces no

branches, and the leaves only iffue from the top, under and among which is the fruit.

PAUSS—one quarter of a day.

PAYER GAUT—the lower pafs.

PAYKASHTA—farmers who cultivate lands by contract, to which they themfelves do not belong.

PEADA—a foot foldier.

PECHE—fortnights.

PEENDA—a cake prefented at the Hindoo temples as an offering on account of the dead: which ceremony is performed on the days of the new and full moon.

PEEPUL—a bitter drug.

PEER—Monday.

PEER—mendicants—monks—teachers.

PEER—a founder or chief of any fects—prior of a Chriftian monaftery—a helper in a tavern, or any houfe of promifcuous entertainment.

PEER MUGHAN—a chief prieft of the Magi, or worfhippers of fire.

PEER DERWISHAN—the fuperior of the dervifes, who are an order of Mahomedan monks.

PEHTEEK—a kind of white ftone.

PEIADAK—a guard to accompany a prifoner at large.

PEISA—cafh.

PEISHACK—one of the three inferior modes of marriage among the Hindoos: it is when a man, coming in difguife of a woman, debauches the girl, and afterwards the parents marry her to the fame.

PEIKUSH—a prefent from an inferior to a prince.

PEONS—foot foldiers: they are employed to affift in collecting the revenues—moft perfons keep fervants who wear a belt with the mafter's name, who are termed peons or puns.

PERAJAPUT—one of the five fuperior modes of marriage: it is when the bridegroom agrees to join when he performs any act of religion.

PERASCHUT—expiation—recovery.

PERBERJA BESHEET—a funiaffy made a flave for apoftacy.

PERE—Monday.

PERGAR—the fairies.

PERGUNNA—a diftrict.

PERKERNUCKA—a fpecies of petty offences.

PERM ATMA—the univerfal foul.

PERRANEK NEEAY—appeal to former decifions.

PERSEES—worfhippers of the elements: they are followers of Zoroafter.

PERSIAN LANGUAGE—there are two forts: the old, called
Zeban-e-Pehlowy; the modern, called Zebaun-e-dery.

PERTUBBISH GUNDEN—acknowledgment of a claim,
but an affertion that it is repaid—an affertion of one
that has a right to a piece of ground, which another,
from the fame caufe, claims a right to.

PERUST—a fmall weight or meafure—four koodups.

PERWANNA—an order—warrant—or a letter figned by
a nawaub.

PESHCUSH—a fine, or fum paid to government as an
acknowledgment for any tenure.

PESHKAR—a fteward.

PESHWA, or PAISHWA—prime minifter—the acting head
of the Mahratta ftates.

PETEEK—a white ftone—cryftal.

PETEL—the head over a village.

PERRIKHAGE—the trial of gold and filver.

PETTAH—a town adjoining a fort, which is in general
furrounded by a fence of bamboos, a wall, and a
ditch.

PHATUK—a gaol or prifon—a gate.

PHAUGUN—a month which in fome degree agrees with
February and March.

PHIRMAUND—fee *Firmaun.*

PHOUSDAR—fee *Foufdar.*

PICE—a copper coin ufed in moft parts of India, but
differing greatly in value.

PIECE GOODS—under this mercantile term, the immenfe
variety of fabrics which are formed of cotton are com-
prehended.

PINDARES—plunderers who accompany a Mahratta
army.

PIPLER—the female banyan-tree: it is very fimilar to one fort of poplar.

PLASS—the name of a tree.

POLLAM—equal to twenty ounces: forty make a viz, in weight, at Madrafs.

POLYGARS—chiefs of mountainous and woody diftriĉts in the peninfula, who pay only a temporary homage.

PONCHUTTRAS—cuftoms.

PONSWAYS—fmall boats.

POOJAY—worfhip to Dewtah the creator of all things.

POOJAY SERSHUTTEE—worfhip to Serfhutte the goddefs of letters.

POOLBUNDY—a dam to prevent inundations.

POOLIAHS—perfons who profefs a fpecies of Mahomedanifm, extremely corrupted by the Indian fuperftitions. The Mahomedan Arabs in India propagated their religion by buying flaves, to whom, after they had been circumcifed, and inftruĉted in their doĉtrine, they gave their freedom; but as a certain pride prevented them from mixing their blood with that of freedmen, the latter in time became a diftinĉt people, inhabiting the coaft of India from Goa, round the peninfula to Madrafs: they go by the above name in Malabar, and by that of Coolies on the Coromandel.

POOLICHEES—a race of men who fuffer ftill greater injuries and hardfhips than the Pariahs: they inhabit the forefts of Malabar, where they are not permitted to build huts, but are obliged to make a kind of neft upon the trees; when they are preffed by hunger they howl, to excite compaffion from thofe paffing; the charitable depofit fome rice, or other food, at the foot of a tree, and retire with all poffible hafte, to give the famifhed wretch an opportunity of taking it without meeting with his benefaĉtor.

POOLUND—a tribe of Hindoos, defcended from a woman of the Bice having had connexion with a man of the Deiool caft.

POONA—a day fixed for the zemindars to bring in their balances for the year.

POONEA—the name of a month.

Poor—at the end of words means *city*.

Pooran—one of the Gentoo fcriptures upon hiftory.

Pooran Shaster—Hindoo hiftories.

Poose—the name of a month following *Ughun* : it in fome meafure agrees with December and January.

Pooshtay Bundee—embankments of rivers—or bridges over rivers.

Pooshte Kerm—prayers for health and profperity.

Pooskul—a fmall weight : eight koonchys.

Pootee—a book, or compilation.

Potta—a leafe.

Potta Chindaree—a cuftom of one rupee given for a leafe, when a piece of ground is bought.

Pottadar—a leafeholder.

Pourie—wooden fandals, ufed during the wet feafon.

Powukkush—a tribe of Hindoos, produced from the connexion of a Bice woman with a man of the Deiool caft : it is their duty to flay wild beafts.

Prakrit—a language ufed by the vulgar.

Pran and Opan—the breathing fpirit—and the fpirit which acteth in the bowels to expel the fæces.

Pra-si-maha-pout—in the Balic language, the tree fa-cred to the great Mercury.

Proa—the name of a failing veffel.

Pucca seer—there are fifteen to a Bombay maund.

Pucka—a putrid fever, generally fatal in twenty-four hours.

Puckallies—leathern bags for carrying water: they are placed on the backs of oxen.

Puddum—one hundred crores.

Puhur Din—diurnal watches : there are four in the day. Thofe of the night, which are alfo four, are called puhur rat.

Pull—a fmall weight or meafure—a meafure of time which is fixty bipull.

Pulwar—a light boat ufed for difpatches.

Pummals—a fruit of the nature of the orange, but much larger, with an extraordinary thick rind : it is called fhaddock in the Weft Indies.

Pulung-teen Choor—the bed of three thieves—the Great Bear conftellation.

Pun—eighty cowries: of the value of about a half-penny.

Punchuck—farmers over and above the fixed revenue.

Pundit—a Shanfcrit word : an honorary title fignifying doctor or philofopher. The pundits are the only men who underftand the Shanfcrit, the language in which the ancient writings of the Hindoos are compofed.

Pungeet—a flave who has loft his liberty as a ftake at fome game.

Pungtee Chhund—in the Shanfcrit is a kind of mea-fured profe: the four Beids, which are erroneoufly faid to be in verfe, are written in this language.

Punjaub—the five waters—the Attock river.

Puntubbee Baden—a falute—or reverence paid by a bride to the bridegroom, at the end of the agammi fhadee, or days of marriage.

Purdaw—a curtain.

Purdesse—a ftranger.

Pubrekeh—trial by ordeal—affay of metals.

Purwarie—the Cocunic name for the Deera caft of Hindoos.

Putny Silk—as produced from the worm after the firft winding off from the pod.

Putwary—an inferior officer of the collections : he keeps the accounts of the rents realized in his village or department, and fettles for them with the muck-adum.

Pykar—a perfon who purchafes goods from the manu-facturer to fell to the merchant.

Pykars—an inferior fort of brokers.

Pyke—a perfon employed as a guard at night.

R

RABAT—is the fame kind of poem as the ghazel, only it docs not exceed five diftichs.

RAGA—an Hindoo god of the mode: one is fuppofed to prefide over each of the fix feafons, into which the Hindoos divide their year; the names are, *Seefar*, *Heemat*, *Vafunt*, *Greefhma*, *Varfa*, and *Sarat*: each raga is attended by five raganies.

RAGANIES—are nymphs of harmony: five attend every raga.

RAGGY—a fmall, but coarfe grain, which abounds in the Myfore and other high countries of India.

RAHADAR—an officer employed in collecting the land duties.

RAHADARY—a tax on the tranfportation of goods.

RAJAH—a title given to Hindoo chiefs: it fignifies prince, and was firft appropriated to the original zemindar.

RAJAH MOODO—the fucceffor elect to the fultaun of Mindano.

RAJAH PRICHUTT—lived in the earlieft ages of the collee jogue : anxious to trace the progrefs of the world from its infancy, he inftigated Shukeh Diew, a learned bramin, fon of Beäfs the author of the Mahabaret, to write the hiftory of India, which work is called Shree Bhagbut.

RAJAPOOTES—a tribe of Hindoos, but of various denominations: they are foldiers by profeffion, and the moft warlike of the Hindoos.

RAKHUS—one of the three inferior modes of marriage : it is when a man marries the daughter of a perfon he has conquered in war.

RAM RAJAH—the head of the Coringo country—or nominal prince or idol of the Mahrattas; the acting power being in the hands of the peifhwa.

RANNA, or RANA—highnefs—prince.

RANNEE—princefs—a title given to women of rank.

RASTABUNDY—making or repairing of the roads.

RATIB—a ftated ration for the fubfiftence of animals.

RAUGS—particular melodies in the Indian mufic; they are fix : the firft five were produced by Mahadeo, from his five heads ; and his wife Parbuttee produced the fixth : they have all miraculous powers attributed to them.

RAUGINEES—are particular melodies in the Indian mufic; they are thirty in number, which were compofed by Brama : miraculous powers are attributed to all of them.

RAZYNAMA—a writing of agreement or concord to end a difpute or litigation.

REBEEWAR—Sunday.

RECAYAH—farmers.

REES—a nominal very fmall coin.

REESHEES—faints.

REKHTU—the mixed dialect of Hindooftan.

RESHEVET—a bride.

RESOOM—fees—or dues.

RHAGOON—the twelfth month, which in fome refpect correfponds with February : it follows the month Magh.

RISSALA, or RUSSAULA—an independent corps of horfe.

RISSALDAR—the commander of the corps of horfe called *riffala*.

RIZAMEDAR—an officer commanding a fmall body of horfe.

RO—in Indian mufic, quick.

ROBIN—a meafure, four of which make a candy.

ROCKET—a war inftrument filled with gunpowder : its form is like an Englifh fkyrocket : it is thrown among the enemy, chiefly at night, to put them into confufion : they go with great force, fo as to reach upwards of a thoufand yards, and to pierce through two perfons. The tube is iron, about a foot long, and an inch in diameter, fixed to a bamboo rod of ten or twelve feet long; fome have a chamber, and burft like a fhell : others, called ground-rockets, have a ferpentine motion, and on ftriking the ground rife again, and bound along till their force is fpent; they make a great noife, and annoy the native cavalry who move in great bodies, but feldom take effect againft our troops, who are formed in lines of great extent and no great depth.

ROHILLAS—a tribe of Afgans inhabiting the country north of the Ganges, as far as the fuba of Oude to the eaftward.

KOIDĀD—reprefentation or ftate of a cafe.

ROKER—cafh.

ROOBAEE—the lighter and fhorter fpecies of poetry, fo called from their being in tetraftichs, more properly called Morubbu.

ROOKN—the term by which Arabians call a metrical foot.

ROURA—lord—fir—mafter—worfhip.

ROWANNA, or ROVINDA—a paffport or certificate from the collector of the cuftoms.

ROXANA—refplendence.

ROY—a Hindoo prince.

ROY ROYAN—the principal officer or comptroller of the kalfa fhreefa.

ROZEENDAR—a perfon holding a yearly penfion.

ROZENADAR—one who receives an allowance daily.

ROZENAMA—a day-book.

ROZIDUS HARAY—certain holydays for fifteen days in the month of Bhadur or Affen, when the worfhip and burial of the Hindoo deities are celebrated.

RUBBY—a feafon of the year: it comprehends the months of Chaite, Byfac, Jeet, Affam, Sohan, and Baudoon. The other half of the year is called Kereef.

RUDEEF—fyllabic additions to the end of a line, for the purpofe of lengthening out the verfe, fuch as our, fir, O, me.

RUFEEU TUKHULLOOS—a poetic furname.

RUJUK—taylors—or wafhers: a tribe of Hindoos which takes its origin from the defcendants of a man of the Kerrun and a woman of the Bice caft.

RUMMUZZAUN—the name of a Mahomedan month.

RUPEE—a filver coin which varies according to the part

of India where they are made: thofe ftruck by the Englifh are generally reckoned of the value of two fhillings and fixpence.

Russoot—a tribe of Hindoos whofe duty it is to take care of horfes.

Russumdar—a perfon holding a particular perquifite.

Rutty—a weight—feven eighths of a carat.

Ryet, or Ryot—the lower order of people, particularly the cultivators of the ground.

Ryet Lands—land farmed out, and cultivated by the tenant.

S

Sabel—proof

Sacontala—an ancient Indian dramatic poem.

Sadhay—certain food and treatment for women in the laft ftate of pregnancy.

Sady—the fortunate.

Safynama—a certificate or writing, fpecifying any matter of difpute to be cleared up and fettled.

Sagh—vegetable.

Sago—a tree of the palm fpecies : a flour is made from this tree, which formed into bread, when frefh from the oven, eats like hot rolls; when hard, it requires being foaked in water before it is ufed. Three of the trees are fufficient to maintain a man a year; and an acre, properly planted, will afford fubfiftence for one hundred for that time.

Sah—a banker.

Saheb—mafter—fir.

Sahooker—a merchant.

Sairjat—all kinds of taxation befides the land rent.

Sairs—any place or office appointed for the collection of duties and cuftoms.

Sakin—immoveable—or intermiffive.
Saladin—the virtue of the faith.
Salam—the compliments of ceremony when perfons meet—in a meffage, refpeɛts—compliments to any one.
Sallaband—ufual cuftom.
Sallesee—arbitration.
Sallis—an arbitrator.
Salmanazer—the falutation of victory.
Salooter—a farrier.
Salooteree—the bufinefs of a farrier.
Sam—the firft of the four books of the Veds, compofed to be chanted or fung.
Samorin—formerly emperor of the country round Ca-licut.
Sampodar—a treafurer, or cafhkeeper.
Sandal—a valuable wood ufed as a perfume.
Saneds, or Sunnuds—commiffions or grants for parti-cular countries.
Sankra—a fuperior among the Talopins or Siamefe priefts: each monaftery has one, who is elected by its members.
Sanskrit—the ancient language of the Hindoos, in which all their religious books are written : it is com-pofed of the word *fan* a prepofition, and *fkrita* done, or finifhed. It is not allowable for any Hindoo to know this language, except thofe of the bramin caft.
Sante Kerm—extraordinary prayers upon any calamity
Sarasootee—the name of one of the fhorteft Shanfcrit grammars: it contains between two and three hun-dred pages, and was compiled by Anoobhootee Seroo-penam Acharige, with a concifenefs that can fcarcely be paralleled in any other language.
Sarat—breaking—the breaking up or ending of the rains.
Sardar—a chief—or leader.
Sarries—a fpecies of cloth.
Sasee—the moon.
Sastra—fee *Shafter*
I

SATMASSA—a fee, paid by married men to the cauzy, after the firſt ſeven months pregnancy of their wives.

SATTELEES—eight make a ſocco at Bencoolen.

SAUL—a timber tree.

SAUT—an hour.

SAUZ—the name of the year 1225, from the birth of Mahomed.

SAWN—the name of a month, which partly correſponds with July.

SAYER—the revenue which ariſes from other things except land.

SAYER PUNCHOOTRA—the cuſtoms collected by government.

SEBOOS—bran.

SEBUNDY—the allowances for charges of an aumil's officers, and thoſe whom he employs.

SEEDEE—the admiral of the Great Mogul—a tribe of Mahomedans in India who came originally from Africa.

SEEKER—a tribe of Hindoos which ſprung from a man of the Magdeh having had connexion with a woman of the Sooder.

SEEKHAUBERDESHY—intereſt to be paid daily.

SEEMUL—a ſpecies of cotton.

SEEPEEYA—a triangle to which culprits are tied to be flogged.

SEER—a weight nearly a pound.

SEESAR—the dewy ſeaſon.

SEEARISH—a recommendation.

SEFFY—a dynaſty of Perſia.

SEJA—a fenced terrace.

SEIKS—a tribe of Hindoos who profeſs deiſm—the word feik means diſciple.

SELAMY—a preſent on being introduced to a ſuperior.

SEPADAR—an officer of the rank of brigadier general.

SEPAHE—a feudatory chief, or military tenant.

SEPHARRY—afternoon.

SEPOYS—derived from Sephaye—natives who have become ſoldiers in the infantry of the Company: theſe forces have both native and European officers, but the Europeans at all times command.

SER—a kind of grafs.

SERADDAY—feaft in honour of the dead.

SERADDAY AMAWAS—a feftival at the end of every lunar month, which is called the night of darknefs.

SERADDAY APERPUK—a preparatory feftival to the rozidus baray, upon the day of Shebbi Tareckee, or night of darknefs, when the fateheh buzurgwar is performed.

SERADDAY BUZURGWAR—a feftival for deceafed anceftors.

SERADDAY NOWANN—an offering made once a year in the month Augun, when rice, milk, fugar, candy, ripe plantains, yam, cocoa-nut, ginger, and fugar-candy are offered, and the fateheh buzurgwar is performed.

SERAF—fee *Shrof.*

SERAI—a building in different divifions, built for paffengers : and perfons are generally appointed by the government to attend there.

SERAGLIO—the women's apartments.

SERAKHUR—the mafter of the horfe.

SERANGS—native officers employed in the artillery and in fhips.

SERASKUR—commander in chief of the Turkifh army.

SERHUD—a boundary—or frontier.

SERINDAH—a mufical inftrument, fomething like the violin in form, but it has only three ftrings, which are of a certain kind of filk.

SERINJAMY KURCH—charges of collection.

SERPAW—a garment, which is prefented by a fuperior in token of protection, and fometimes by inferiors in token of homage.

SERSHEKEN—a free grant of a mahal to any perfon, the rents of which are made up by an additional affeffment on the refidue of the lands.

SERWAESHER—lord of all—is that omnifcience which is centred in the fpirit of God.

SERWATTERRE—a bramin learned in the Beids.

SETENDY—militia.

SET,H—a banker.

SEWARRY—the train of attendants who accompany their mafter—and alfo the cattle.

SEWY—the increafe of the rents of the jaghire lands.

SEZAWEL—an officer employed to collect the revenues.

SHABAUN—the name of a Mahomedan month.

SHADAUB—the name of the year 1226 from the birth of Mahomed.

SHAGHUR—a deity of the Hindoos.

SHAGURD PESHA—retinue—fervants.

SHAH—mendicants—monks—teachers.

SHAHEE—a fmall coin, of the value of about three-pence.

SHAHER—city.

SHAHESH—violence.

SHAIKDAR—a perfon, who, from his reverential appearance, is applied to as magiftrate.

SHAIT—bridges—embankments.

SHALLEE—fee Batty.

SHANSCRIT—fee Sanfkrit.

SHAROCH—a filver coin of about one fhilling value.

SHARUK—a tribe, which fprung from a man of the Malakar caft having connexion with a woman of the Sooder caft.

SHASTER—the fcriptures of the Hindoos—in particular, books on fcience.

SHAUMIARAS—a canopy of cotton cloth.

SHAW—king.

SHAW ALLUM—king of the world.

SHAW BUNDER—the king's cuftom-houfe.

SHAWZADA—the king's fon.

SHEBBY DEIJORE—nights in which the moon does not appear.

SHEBBY TERECKY—nights in which the moon only fhines for a fhort time.

SHEED—a witnefs.

SHEERTEE—a certain part of the Hindoo fcriptures, containing the code of moral and religious law which the Hindoos obferve.

SHEIK—a caft of Mahomedans.

SHEKDAR—a collector of revenues.

SHEMABHEE—games of fighting animals.

SHEPAA—a Hindoo caft, originating from a connexion between a Kayta and a Wookree.

SHER MOOHUMMUD—the tiger of Mahomy.

SHERAKUT-I-BRADEREE—that kind of partnerfhip where all the brothers or members of a family live together, have a joint ftock, and are coheirs in all inheritances left to the family.

SHERAKUT-I-TEJARUTEE—partnerfhip in trade.

SHEREEF—noble—magnificent.

SHERISCHER-WAR—Saturday.

SHERISTA—an office—or regiftry.

SHERISTADAR—the office or regifter keeper.

SHERRUNKAR—jewellers—or goldfmiths : a tribe of Hindoos, produced by the connexion of a man of the Ambufht and a woman of the Bice caft

SHET AGHNEE—the Shanfcrit word for cannon—or the weapon that kills a hundred men at once; from *fhete*, a hundred, and *gheneh*, to kill.

SHISH—a ftudent.

SHOBERUN BINEIK, or SOONAR BUNEEAH—a tribe of Hindoos, which took its rife from the defcendants of a man of the Ambufht and a woman of the Bice caft: their office is the trial of gold and filver.

SHOCCA—any letter written by the king.

SHOOKEH—a tribe of Hindoos, who are defcended from a Bice woman having had connexion with a man of the Deiool caft.

SHOOKREWAR—Friday.

SHOONDRUK, or SHODRIE—a tribe defcended from a man of the Koop and a woman of the Sooder caft.

SHREE BHAGHUT—a hiftory of India : a work compofed four thoufand years ago, by Shukeh Diew, a learned bramin: it treats of the hiftory of India through the three preceding jogues or ages, giving the fucceffion of the feveral rajahs, and the duration of their reigns ; it is divided into twelve afkund or books, and three thoufand and twenty chapters.

SHROF—a banker—money-changer.

SHROFFING—examining and forting money.

SHUKERAUNA—a fee paid by the plaintiff or defendant, on his caufe being determined in his favour.

SHUKESTEH—one of the three methods of writing among the Perfians.

SHUMSERTREE PUT—confeffion—acknowledgment.

SHUNKEREE KURRUM—the act of flaying an animal.

SHUTERNAUL—a kind of harquebufs fixed on the back of a camel.

SHUWAUL—the name of a month.

SICCA—any coin—a feal.

SIDDY—lord—fee *Seedee*.

SIES, or SHIAS—a tribe of people in the N.W. of India.

SIGURGHAL—a feudal tenure.

SINASSEE—one who having affumed the braminical thread, cuts and fhaves the hair from his head, burns the braminical thread, and clothing himfelf in two red cloths, and carrying a bamboo ftaff of his own height in his right hand, and an earthen pot in his left, forfakes his wife and children and becomes a fakeer.

SIRGHATTY MEHAL—a fair for horned cattle.

SIRI, SIRI, RAM—a form of invocation of God among the Hindoos put at the beginning of all writings.

SIRJA—a certain kind of drefs.

SIRKAR—the government.

SKANDA, or KARTEEK—the general of the celeftial armies.

SOHAN—the feventh month : it in fome meafure agrees with July and Auguft.

SOM—a creeper: the juice of which is commanded to be drunk at the conclufion of a facrifice, by the perfon for whom, and at whofe expenfe it is performed, and by the bramins who officiate at the altar.

SOME WAR—Monday.

SOOCIES—a fpecies of filk cloth.

SOOD—intereft.

SOODER—the fourth or loweft of the original tribes of the Hindoos, as they come from the feet of Brama, which fignifies fubjection : they are to labour and ferve.

Soofee—mendicants—monks—teachers.

Sookrbar—Friday.

Soonar Buneeah—fee *Shoberun bineik.*

Soondrie—fee *Shoondruk.*

Soontaburdar—an attendant, who carries a filver club before his mafter: he is inferior to the chubdar.

Sooradhuck—a mark of infamy to be branded in the forehead of a bramin for drinking wine.

Soorethaul—reprefentation or ftatement of a cafe.

Soors—good angels.

Sooskanell—the name given to one of the revolutions of twelve years.

Soot—i. e. fellers of flowers : a tribe compofed originally of the production from the connexion between a man of the Chehtree and a woman of the Bramin caft.

Soparie—the tree on which the nut called *betel* grows— the tree fimilar to the cocoa-nut, excepting that it never grows fo thick.

Soukars—bankers.

Soudagree—merchandife.

Soudagur—a merchant.

Sour—a nickname.

Soura—a divifion, as that of chapter.

Sowar—a horfeman.

Sowauree Khauss—the fpecial retinue.

Sowgund—an oath.

Stable-Horse—that part of Tippoo Sultaun's cavalry which are beft armed, accoutred, and moft regularly difciplined.

Suba—a province.

Subadar—the governor of a province over other nawaubs, as the fubadar of the Decan, who receives from the feveral nawaubs the crown rents, and remits them to the treafury of the empire—alfo a black officer, who in the Company's forces ranks as a captain, but never can command when an European officer is prefent.

Subadary—the office of a fubadar.

Subub khufeep—a fort of half foot—a cæfura.

2

SUBUB SUQUEEL—a term in the Indian profody anfwering to that of pyrrhichius.

SUDARA—the birth of a crocodile, as a brother to a newborn infant, which the inhabitants of Java fuppofe to take place; and they imagine that the midwife conveys the young crocodile to an adjacent river, into which fhe puts it with the utmoft care and tendernefs. Thofe who fuppofe themfelves honoured by the birth of this new relation, fail not to put food in the river for his fubfiftence. In the iflands of Bouton and Celebes the natives keep crocodiles in their families, and it is conjectured, that the ftrange idea of the twin crocodile was firft conceived there; it extends however among the iflands to the eaftward as far as Ceram and Timor.

SUDDUR—chief.

SUDDUR CAUZEE—the chief or head cauzee.

SUDDUR UL HUCK—chief adminiftrator of juftice at Lucknow.

SUFFUR—the name of a month.

SULTAN—king—the title affumed by Tippoo the chief of the Myfore country.

SULTAN SHIRKI—king of the Eaft.

SULTANUT—the appendages to a monarch.

SUMNUTCHEER—Saturday.

SUMOODER—the fea—or main ocean.

SUMPERTEE PUTT—is when a man producing a claim upon another, the perfon anfwers, " I confefs that the fubject of your claim is in my poffeffion;" in this cafe there is no need of writing or witnefs.

SUN—the year.

SUNAT—old rupees on which a difcount is allowed.

SUNEEBAR—Saturday.

SUNEECHUR—Saturday.

SUNGSERSUT—a fecond formation of a family connexion.

SUNIASSIES—fee *Sinaffee*.

SUNKAKAR—or artificers in funkha or fea-fhells: a tribe of Hindoos who were originally produced from the connexion between a Bice woman and a bramin.

SUNKHA—a fea-fhell commonly called chank.

Sunnud—a charter, grant, or patent, from any man in authority : when from the king it is called a *firmaun*.

Sunnud Dewauny—a grant or writing for holding land.

Surapan—an honorary drefs conferred on an inferior by a fuperior.

Surdar—the name given to thofe who are employed to wind filk.

Surut Haal—a ftate of the cafe.

Suttee—the fixth of the fpheres above the earth, is the refidence of Brama, and his particular favourites— this is the place of deftination for thofe men who have never uttered a falfehood; and for thofe women who have voluntarily burned themfelves at the death of their hufbands.

Suttee Jogue—or age of purity, is, according to the Hindoos, the firft of the four æras or periods of Indian chronology : it is faid to have exifted three millions two hundred thoufand years, and that the life of man was extended, in that age, to one hundred thoufand years, and that his ftature was twenty-one cubits— (Mr. Halhed.) Mr. Roger fays the futtee jogue is a period of one million feven hundred and twenty-eight thoufand years. Mr. Bernier fays, it was two millions five hundred thoufand years.

Swammies—pagan gods or idols.

Swergeh—one of the fix fpheres above the earth : the Hindoos call it the firft paradife, and general receptacle for thofe who merit a removal from the lower earth.

Syed—a caft of Mahomedans—the defcendants of Fatimah the daughter of Mahomed.

Syef—a long fword.

Syeful Mulk—the fword of the kingdom.

T

TAGABEY—money lent at intereſt to a huſbandman, to enable him to cultivate his land : for payment of which the enſuing crop is bound.

TAGHEEREE—diſmiſſion.

TAGUR—the domeſtic idol of Hindoo adoration.

TAHUD—an agreement, or leaſe, or contract, on the part of the leſſor.

TAJEE—the performer of the journies of the kundherps, or good ſpirits, is a horſe of the Perſian race.

TAIGAU—a ſabre.

TALE—equal to ſix ſhillings and eight-pence.

TALICK—one of the three methods of writing the Perſian character.

TALOOK, or TALOOKDARY—a leaſe in perpetuity—a ſmall zemindary.

TALOOKDAR—the head of any department under a ſuperior.

TALOPINS—Siameſe prieſts.

TALY—a gold ornament which married women wear round their neck : at the time of the marriage ceremony, the woman's father gives this ornament to the bridegroom, who puts it round the neck of the woman, and they are married.

TAMOUL—a dialect of the Hindooſtany language uſed on the Coromandel coaſt.

TANIJANS—ſpotted horſes brought to Hindooſtaun for ſale : they are of a hardy race.

TANK—a pond or pool of water—a reſervoir to preſerve the water that falls during the rainy ſeaſon : moſt houſes have one, and all pagodas, and muſſeeds.

TANKA—the revenue appropriated by the Mogul for the maintenance of a fleet at Surat to protect the merchants and Mahomedan pilgrims going to Mecca.

TANKSALL—a mint.

TANNADAR—a commander of a ſmall fort.

TAPPEE—an exprefs.

TAPROBANE—the ancient name for the ifland of Ceylon, which is derived from *tapoo*, an ifland, and *bany*, a ferry.

TAREJE—an account fpecifying the particulars, and afterwards the addition.

TASA—a kind of drum, formed from a femifphere of copper, hollowed out and covered with goat-fkin; it is hung before from the fhoulders, and beat with two rattans.

TASILDAR—an officer employed at a monthly falary to collect the revenues.

TASSEEL—collection of revenue.

TATTA—a wood very fimilar to the elder, but of much quicker growth and weaker.

TATTA—a bamboo frame, which enclofes a herb called jawaffea : they are made to put to the different openings of a room; thefe having water thrown againft them, the hotteft wind in paffing through becomes cool.

TATTOOS—a fmall inferior fpecies of horfes.

TAUDIDAUDS—literally, affets; but applied to affignments.

TAUNTY—the caft of weavers.

TAWLEEK, or TILLEE—a tribe produced from the connexion of a Bice man and a woman of the Sooder caft : the employment of this tribe is to fell beetel nut.

TAZEE—a deformed race of horfes.

TCHAGUL—a leather bottle to hold water.

TCHOLI KA BAJEE—a fort of greens fimilar to fpinage.

TEEK—the name of a wood with which moft furniture and ftrong buildings are made, and all the fhips of India; it lafts much longer than oak.

TEEK—careful of money—ftingy.

TEEP—a contract—or note of hand.

TEEP—a term in Indian mufic, fignifying that the note is to be raifed an octave.

TELINGY—a fepoy—a dialect ufed on the Coromandel coaft.

TELISM—a charm—or talifman.

TEILKAR—makers and fellers of oil : a tribe of Hindoos, produced from a man of the Koop having connexion with a woman of the Sooder.

TERHARREE—greens.

TERREGEY—law of divifion of property.

TERUR—a fee for writing.

TESSIDUCK, or ISAR—a ceremony ufed upon the accef-fion of a prince to the throne; the omrahs running three times round the king, waving an offering of mo-ney, in a charger, three times over the monarch's head : this money, like all other offerings, is after-wards delivered over to the almoner to be diftributed in charity.

TEVEEL—the treafury.

TEVEELDAR—a treafurer.

THAKOOR—lord—fir—mafter—worfhip.

THECK—a thing made with fplit bamboos, to hang to a window to prevent impertinent curiofity; the fticks, each of which reach acrofs the window, about the thicknefs of a ftraw, are joined together by means of ftring.

THEEKAANA—the place where any perfon is either a fojourner or inhabitant.

THURRAH—a term in Indian mufic fignifying, double; but not fo quick as to be confounded into one.

TIKEN—a kind of cloth.

TIL, or UNOOPUL—a meafure of time : fixty of which make a bipul, which is the twenty-fourth part of a minute.

TILLEE—fee *Tawleck.*

TINDALS—native officers employed in the artillery and in fhips.

TIRTAH JOGUE—fucceeds the futtee jogue, and is the fecond of the four æras or periods of Indian chrono-logy. In this age one third of mankind was corrupted; it is fuppofed to have lafted two million four hundred thoufand years, and that men lived to the age of ten thoufand years—(Mr. Halbed.) Mr. Roger fays, it is one million two hundred and ninety-fix thoufand; Mr. Bernier fays, one million two hundred thoufand years; Colonel Dow, one million eighty thoufand years.

TIUMMUM—a purification by fprinkling duft over the body.

TIWAREE—the title of a clafs of bramins.

TODDY—the fermented juice of the date or palmyra tree.

TOFFAUL—a collection of calarries or falt-pans.

TOHIE—a canoe.

TOKERY—a bafket made with cane.

TOLAS—thirty-two—thirteen volls make twelve ounees.

TOLECHAY—a weight, containing ten mafhays of filver, and twelve of gold.

TOMAN—ten thoufand men.

TOMAND—equal to fomething more than three guineas.

TOMAR JUMMA—the original amount of revenue, fettled on a meafurement of the lands.

TOMSOOK HAZIR ZAMINEE—a fecurity for perfonal appearance.

TOMTOM—a drum of the fhape of a tambourine.

TOOKSOWARS—the vizier's body of horfe.

TOOMRIE—a mufical inftrument in form of a globe, with the axis extended from the oppofite fides : it is made from a dried bauberie, hollowed out, the ftem of which forms a mouth-piece; on the oppofite fide, two bamboo pipes of equal length are inferted, one of which has fix holes on one fide, and one on the other; the other bamboo has one hole near the bottom ; in the infide of the bauberie two reeds are inferted into the bamboo, which are fplit fo as to form valves.

TOPASS—a native Portuguefe foldier : the natives of India gave them this name on account of their wearing hats.

TOOP—a fmall wood or grove.

TOOP E WALLA—a perfon who wears a hat: it means an European in converfe.

TOOP CONNA—the place where the guns, &c. are kept.

TOSHA CONNA—ftore-room—wardrobe.

TOWJEE—monthly ftatements of the collections.

TRIPAM—a fpecies of mufhroom which grows in the ifland of Celebes: the rounder and blacker it is, the more excellent.

TRIPETY FEAST—fo called from the name of a pagoda where it is annually held.

TUCDUMMA—an account clofed after it has been examined.

TUCKAVY—money lent on intereft to farmers, to enable them to carry on their cultivation.

TUKHULLOOS—the poetic agnomen of an author, exprefled in a fort of verfe called *Muqtu*.

TUKKEH—a caft of Hindoos, the production of a man of the Abheir caft with a woman of the Bice.

TUKKEKYAH—carpenters: a caft of Hindoos, produced by the connexion of a man of the Kerrun and a woman of the Bice caft.

TUKNAR JUMMA—money brought more than once to account.

TULBANUA—a fee, taken by peons when placed as guards over any perfon.

TULLUB—a demand—often ufed as pay.

TULLUB CHITTY—a fummons.

TULWAR—a fword.

TUMBOOLEE—feller of the betel-leaf: a caft of Hindoos which arofe from the defcendants of a woman of the Sooder and a man of the Bice caft.

TUMBRELS—covered carts which carry ammunition for the cannon.

TUMUSSOOK—a bond.

TUNCAW—an affignment.

TUNTERBA—weavers: a caft of Hindoos, which takes its origin from a connexion between a man of the Sooder and a woman of the Chehtree.

TUPPEH—is, according to the Hindoos, the fifth fphere above the earth: thofe who have all their lives performed fome wonderful act of penance and mortification, or who have died martyrs to their religion, go there.

TURB—radifhes.

TURJEE BUND—thofe poems which have a returning line, or chorus, repeated at diftinct intervals.
TUSHBAY CONNAY—an oratory where prayers are faid.
TUSSULDAR—the Company's collector of the kifty-bunds.
TYER—four cream.

P

VAJIB UL ARZEE—a petition or propofal to a fuperior.
VAKEEL—an agent—an inferior ambaffador.
VAKEEL MUTTULUCK—fee *Muttuluck Vakeel*.
VAKIAS—a weight, nearly fimilar to a pound—it is alfo a meafure.
VAKILIT—the firft office in the empire.
VAROON—the Hindoo god of the ocean.
VARSA—the rainy feafon.
VASANT—the mild feafon—or fpring.
VASOODY—the father of Kreefhna in his incarnation.
VASORS—eight of the firft beings created by Brama.
VAYOO—the Hindoo god of the winds.
UBDOOLLAH—the flave of God—fee *Abdallah*.
VEDANT—a metaphyfical treatife on the nature of God, which teacheth that matter is a mere delufion; the fuppofed author of which is Vyas.
VEDS—books written by Brihma, treating of the duties of the Hindoo cafts: thefe books he gave to Brama with the power to read and explain them.
VENA—the Indian lute: it is fuppofed to have been invented by Nared the fon of Brihma.
VERANDA—the covering of houfes being extended beyond the main pile of building, by means of a flanting roof, forming external rooms, or paffages.
VETTESSA—the god of riches, otherwife called Koover:

3

he is faid to prefide over the regions of the north, and to be the chief of the Yakfhas and Rakfhas, two fpecies of good and evil genii.

UGHUN—the name of a month which partly correfponds with November: it follows Katik.

VINATEGA—a bird fabled to be of wonderful fize, and the vehicle of Vifhnu.

VIZ—a fmall coin—it is alfo a weight equal to about three pounds: but differs much in value according to place.

VIZARUT—the office of vizeer.

VIZEER—the prime minifter.

ULTUMGAU—a grant of land free from rent, under the royal feal—a gift to the religious or learned.

UMWULLID, or AM UL WULLED—a female flave, who having born a child to her mafter, becomes free.

UNOOPUL—or TIL—a meafure of time: fixty make a bipul, which is the twenty-fourth part of a minute.

VOLLS—forty make a tola.

VREEHASPATEE—the preceptor of the devs or dews—the planet Jupiter—and dies Jovis.

VROOT—a braminical religious office.

USARH—the name of a month, which partly correfponds with our month of June: it follows Jet,h.

USUD ULLEE—the lion of Ullee.

VYAS—the compiler of the Mahabarat.

UZEEZ ULLAH—dear of God.

W

WADA, or WADADARY—a farm of a diftrict.

WADABUNDY—ftated dates, on which money is to be paid.

WADADAR—a government officer, who is refponfible for the rents of a zemindary.

WAKANAGUR—a writer of occurrences.

WALAJAH—exalted in rank.

WARIS—heir.

WASBA—a horfe of the deformed Tazee race : he is the performer of the journies of the jins or demons.

WASELAAT—collections made.

WASEL BAKY—collections and balances.

WASSYOUT NAMA—a will.

WAUGERY—a bird-catcher.

WAYWODE—a prince—chieftain.

WILBE—guardian—protector.

WOHKEELE—an ambaffador.

WOOKREE—the daughter of a Chehtree begotten on a Sooder woman.

WROOT—fee *Vroot.*

WUHAH—fandals.

WULANDA, or WULANDEZ—the Dutch.

WURD—the female banyan-tree.

WURUN—fee *Burrun.*

WUSOOLE—that may be realized or collected.

WUTUD MUJM'OO,U, or MUQROON—in the profody, a triliteral fyllable, with the two moveable letters near or joined to each other.

WUTTUD MUFROOQ—is the term, in verfe, trochæus.

WUZZOO—a purification by fprinkling water over the body.

Y

YAB—a filent repetition of the name of God.

YAD DASHT—a memorandum.

YAM—the judge of hell.

YEHOODY—a Jew.

YESAWUL—a ftate meffenger—a fervant of parade, who carries a filver or gold ftaff—an aid-de-camp.

YETESAB—an officer for regulating weights.
YEZID—excellent—noble.
YOG—junction—or union.
YOU AND WE—a found of falutation, given to ladies of high rank in the ifland of Mindano.

Z

ZAAT—caft—or divifion of people into tribes or fects.
ZAYM—a feudal chief—or military tenant.
ZEBANBUNDY—a depofition.
ZEEARUT—a confecrated fpot.
ZEID—a name ufed in law, as a fuppofed perfon.
ZEINAUB—a word of diftinction ufed to perfons of eminence.
ZELA—fee Zilla.
ZELADAR—fee Zilladar.
ZEMEEN—ground.
ZEMEENDAR—a perfon who holds a tract of land immediately from the government: fomewhat fimilar to a lord of the manor.
ZEMEENDARY—the lands of a zemeendar.
ZENA—fornication—adultery.
ZENAKAN—a perfon committing adultery or fornication.
ZENANA—the women's apartment: always feparate from the others.
ZENNAR—a facred ftring worn by the three higher cafts of the Hindoos : it is hung round the body from the left fhoulder; it is made with a particular kind of perennial cotton, called nerma, compofed of a certain number of threads of a fixed length. That worn by the Khatry caft has fewer threads than that worn by the Bramins, and the Bice have fewer ftill; but the Sooder caft are not permitted to wear it.
ZERAHET—agriculture.

ZERB—a blow or ftroke.
ZERB SHALLAAK—a blow with a ftick.
ZERDUSHT—Zoroafter.
ZEREBAAR—overburdened with expenfes—or borne down with oppreffion.
ZILLA—a diftrict, in fize about a quarter of a pergunna.
ZILLADAR—an officer of the collections.
ZIMMUM—the indorfement of a grant.
ZIMRA—a certificate.
ZINDIGEE—grain—cattle—lands—and plantations.
ZIYAMUT—a fief beftowed for military fervices.
ZOOLFECKAR CAUN—lord of the deftroying weapon.
ZUKKOOM—the name of a tree.
ZULLUM—oppreffion—violence.
ZUNANEE ZUBAAN—the ftyle or dialect of fpeech peculiar to the women of Hindooftaun, which is confidered as unbecoming in a man to ufe.
ZUNNAR—fee *Zennar*.
ZUNNARDAR—the wearer of the zennar.
ZUROOREAT—neceffaries.

THE END.

Printed by S. GOSNELL,
Little Queen Street, Holborn.